# Coaching Skills for Leaders in the Workplace

Visit our How To website at **www.howto.co.uk**

At **www.howto.co.uk** you can engage in conversation with our authors –
all of whom have 'been there and done that' in their specialist fields. You
can get access to special offers and additional content but most
importantly you will be able to engage with, and become a part of, a
wide and growing community of people just like yourself.

At **www.howto.co.uk** you'll be able to talk and share tips with people
who have similar interests and are facing similar challenges in their lives.
People who, just like you, have the desire to change their lives for the
better – be it through moving to a new country, starting a new business,
growing their own vegetables, or writing a novel.

At **www.howto.co.uk** you'll find the support and encouragement you
need to help make your aspirations a reality.

You can go direct to **www.coaching-skills-for-leaders-in-the-work
place.co.uk** which is part of the main How To site.

**How To Books** strives to present authentic, inspiring,
practical information in their books. Now, when you buy a
title from **How To Books,** you get even more than just words
on a page.

# Coaching Skills for Leaders in the Workplace

*How to develop, motivate and get the best from your staff*

Jackie Arnold

**howto**books

Published by How To Books Ltd,
Spring Hill House, Spring Hill Road,
Begbroke, Oxford OX5 1RX. United Kingdom.
Tel: (01865) 375794. Fax: (01865) 379162.
info@howtobooks.co.uk
www.howtobooks.co.uk

How To Books greatly reduce the carbon footprint of their books by sourcing their
typesetting and printing in the UK.

British Library Cataloguing in Publication Data
A catalogue record for this book is available from the British Library

ISBN 978 1 84528 318 6

Produced for How To Books by Deer Park Productions, Tavistock, Devon.
Typeset by PDQ Typesetting, Newcastle-under-Lyme, Staffs.
Printed and bound by Cromwell Press Group, Trowbridge, Wiltshire

NOTE: The material contained in this book is set out in good faith for general guidance
and no liability can be accepted for loss or expense incurred as a result of relying in
particular circumstances on statements made in the book. Laws and regulations are
complex and liable to change, and readers should check the current position with the
relevant authorities before making personal arrangements.

# Contents

# List of figures and tables

## Figures

## Table

This book is dedicated to my mother, Pamela Alice Forsyth, who has always supported me in anything I have put my hand to. Her unfailing belief in me and her willingness always to be there for me have had an incredibly positive influence on my life.

# Acknowledgements

To my family for their continued encouragement and enthusiasm. To my agent, Fiona Spenser Thomas, for her help and support. To Julia Miles of Quality Education and Development, Brighton, who developed many of the ideas and materials contained in this book, for her unfailing patience, support and generosity. I should also like to thank Alison Haill, Oxford Professional Consulting, for her professional and supportive collaboration, and Helen Acklam, Red Starfish, for her companionship, insightful encouragement and gentle nudging!

Grateful thanks also go to the Institute of Leadership and Management Level 5 'Coaching and mentoring' course candidates throughout the UK for their pearls of wisdom and support. To members of the European Growth Group for the wonderful open spaces, professional conversations, ongoing development and spiritual harmony we create all over Europe. To the following supportive coaches and supervisors: Richard Acklam, Fiona Adamson, Bill Bryson, Laura Bergman Fortgang, Julie Hay, Edna Murdock, Miriam Orriss, Ann A. Rushton and Marian Way.

## CASE STUDIES/INTERVIEWS

Lucy Backhurst, Newcastle University.
Sarah Fearon, Head of History, Gosforth High School.
Ghislaine Gauthier, Managing Director, Enhance, Paris.
Tim Gibson, Head of Command and Operational Training, Kent Fire and Rescue Service.
Liz Macann, Head of Coaching Development, BBC, London.
Edna Murdock, Coaching Supervision Academy.
Helen Pringle, Walbottle Campus, Newcastle upon Tyne.

Sam Sheppard, Coral Ingleton, Katie Chantler and Nicky Whichelow, Kent County Council.

Marian Way, clean language coach/trainer, Apricot Island

# Introduction

As a leader, senior manager or executive, you are often required to act as a coach or mentor for your staff. This book will enable you to set up robust coaching programmes that can make a significant difference to staff retention and motivation. It will give you the knowledge and skills you need to encourage your staff to grow so that you can get on with your own essential leadership role.

People often join or set up a business because they have a specific set of skills. After a few years, these skills often bear no relation to the positions they find themselves in. Promotion has seen them rise in the company and suddenly they are faced with managing or leading a team of people. When you have built up a business, you feel responsible for it. This brings with it many challenges. There is a reluctance to let go and trust others to carry out even minor tasks.

Michael E. Gerber, in his series of *E-myth* books, suggests that you need to create a business (or business unit) that works apart from you and not so much because of you. He describes this as working on your business projects and not becoming caught up with merely working in your business. Instead of being consumed by the systems and processes, you nurture your business so that it supports you. This enables you to experience the joy and satisfaction you desired in the first place. As a good manager of people, therefore, it is vital to recognise that others often have greater, more relevant skills than you.

At the International Coaching Federation's (ICF) first European conference in Grindlewald, Switzerland, in 2001, Tim Gallwey (author of the *Inner Game* series of books and a pioneer of coaching) coached four total beginners at tennis using what he referred to as 'self-directed learning' –

a way of enabling people to play a sport using their own internal knowledge and encouraged by a specific set of questions. Gallwey started by explaining that, as babies, no one teaches us how to walk. Parents don't say 'So, here's how you walk. You place one foot forward and then shift your weight so that you can balance and then bring the other foot forward...' and so on. So how do we learn? Simply by watching and observing how others do it. By being encouraged, by having the support of those around you and by being very self-motivated. As Gallwey began to help people play tennis there was no instruction on how to hold the racquet or how to stand. All he did was to encourage people to take part and ask a series of simple questions, such as the following:

- Where do you want the ball to go?
- Do you feel comfortable holding the racquet?
- How fast is the ball travelling?
- If the racquet is facing that way, where will the ball go?

He was just there in the background, encouraging and very gently asking key questions.

At the end of one hour all four players were hitting the ball over the net. They had gained confidence and, despite their initial misgivings, had grasped the basics in a very short time. All of them enjoyed the experience and wanted to continue.

Although similar skills are employed in both coaching and mentoring, this book is mainly for those who would like to find out how effective coaching can be in the workplace. It will also be of value to those wishing to take the Institute of Leadership and Management (ILM) Certificate and Diploma in Coaching and Mentoring in Management at Levels 5 and 7. It focuses on the challenges you will face when trying to balance the dual roles of manager or leader and coach.

You may be wondering exactly what an effective coach does. At the ICF conference mentioned above, Gallwey was asked this question and his reply was very simple. He said that it was the job of the coach to recognise that all the knowledge and solutions were inside the individual being coached and as long as we (and they) look externally for the answers, these will be elusive. Coaches use very specific skills and strategies built up with experience but, in essence, they work with the knowledge and potential the coachee already has. It is up to the coach to nurture and encourage that individual potential. Another comment I have always remembered was that unless we, as coaches, look (and learn from) our own inner wisdom and guidance, we, too, will not be effective in our own lives or when coaching others.

As a leader in the workplace you may question whether you will always be effective as a coach. You may confront challenges in the areas of trust, confidentiality and power differences. Coaching is, to a great extent, a particular mindset and way of behaving. The process works best in a calm and relaxed atmosphere where both parties can be totally focused on what is happening at the present moment. This may not always be appropriate or useful, particularly when quick decisions need to be taken and guidance is essential. Coaching will only be effective in the workplace when there is an atmosphere of openness and honest communication.

It is, however, without doubt the most powerful way of 'being' with, and of nurturing the potential in, others I have ever come across. Transpersonal coaching is now emerging and this has evolved as a result of coaches exploring more of the psychological and spiritual aspects of coaching. I believe it is also the result of companies recognising that employees are motivated by having health and well-being high on the list of company values. Healthy and happy staff stay in role and this saves money on recruitment and training.

A study by the International Personnel Management Association noted that ordinary training typically increased productivity by 22%, while training combined with coaching increased productivity by 88%. Companies such as British Telecom, Ernst & Young, Kodak, the Britannia Building Society and Unilever, to mention a few, are now employing the principles of coaching and mentoring to help with staff development. Through the ILM Centre for Quality Education and Development based in Brighton, Kent County Council and Kent Fire Service have trained over 50 of their senior staff to be workplace coaches. Newcastle City Council has so far trained over 25.

As a manager or leader in the workplace, you will know how vital it is to motivate your teams and enhance the skills of the people you lead. Part of your role is to help and encourage your team to be successful. By using coaching skills in the workplace, you will support your team members to take ownership and responsibility for their actions. As a leader it is easy to give suggestions and to jump in when the answers are clear. However, allowing people to come up with their own solutions and to work out their own strategies is far more empowering. Your people need room to grow and make mistakes without feeling pressured.

By employing coaching skills you will be able to challenge individuals when they falter. Asking open (what? when? where? why? how? who?) and incisive questions encourages them to explore different ways of addressing a problem and to think creatively. Additionally, if you build on the success of each individual, it will inspire them to even greater achievements. This in turn will increase their morale and boost their self-confidence.

# What is coaching?

Coaching is a way of encouraging and supporting someone to achieve a goal or to develop or acquire skills. The focus of coaching is the individual being coached (the coachee). The coach makes interventions to support the coachee to move forward and to take responsibility for their own decisions and actions. Although a coach need not have knowledge or expertise in any areas of their coachees' work, they are skilled professionals trained in methods and processes that enable their coachees to develop and change positively.

A coach creates a particular energy when working with their coachees by being a non-judgemental listener and reflector of the ideas and issues that arise. They do not put forward their own ideas and suggestions during the coaching session. Instead, they remain totally convinced of the potential of those they coach. This enables the coachees to discover and explore hidden areas and to build on their inherent ability for development. Coaching focuses, for the most part, on the present situation and future possibilities.

## EXTERNAL COACHING

External coaches are asked to come into a company to improve individual and business performance. They may have no previous knowledge of the company concerned but are highly skilled in

1

supporting behavioural change and understanding business processes. They may also hold qualifications or have experience in the following areas:

- Neuro-linguistic programming (NLP).
- Personality assessments.
- Setting up 360° feedback.
- Managing change/acquisitions.

## INTERNAL COACHING

Internal coaches are those people who support their own staff or staff from other departments in the same organisation. They may be experienced in coaching or mentoring and may or may not have formal qualifications. An internal coach or mentor will also have knowledge about the successes, failures and challenges their organisation is facing. This can be a great advantage but may also get in the way of successful coaching, as you will see in later chapters.

One of the most common questions asked about coaching is how it differs from other interventions, such as mentoring, counselling and teaching. The following is a summary of the key differences.

## MENTORING

While mentoring and coaching have moved closer over the past ten years, most people agree that a mentor acts as a guide who assists an individual to learn faster and more effectively than they might do alone. An effective mentor will use a range of skills and techniques to allow an individual to obtain a clearer picture of an organisation and their role in it. They may give advice and direction and are usually experienced in their mentees' work. They encourage questions and help their mentees to build up a sense of how their mentees' careers might develop. In this way a vision of what is possible may emerge for the mentee, and they gain confidence in their role and a renewed sense of purpose. A mentor can be particularly helpful for people new to a role or for those looking to gain knowledge and skills from a more experienced colleague.

## COUNSELLING/THERAPY

Counsellors and therapists explore specific, deeper, underlying personal issues and problems. They are trained to use interventions that go to the heart of an issue. Because these issues can be greatly influenced by events in the past, counsellors often look beyond the individual for a solution. In direct contrast to coaching, they avoid putting the burden of responsibility for the problems onto the individual. Instead they use skills and interventions that enable the individual to view things from a different perspective. They encourage people to move forward positively using a range of specialised techniques.

Coaches/mentors should be very aware of when a session is moving into personal, psychological and emotional areas and should maintain strong boundaries. Some coaches may be trained in psychology, psychotherapy or counselling. In this case they may draw on their skills and knowledge in a coaching situation. However, it is important that they clarify with their coachee when they are moving into a therapeutic area/role and gain their coachee's agreement before proceeding in this direction. Generally it is not advisable to move into this second role even when professionally trained – usually a referral to a therapist is a better option. Sometimes coaching may cease so that the person can have therapeutic treatment, but it is possible for someone to be receiving both coaching and counselling concurrently.

Coaching is not appropriate when a client has any of the following:

- Experience of trauma, or physical, mental or sexual abuse.
- Addictions, dependencies or misuse (alcohol, drugs, gambling, etc.).
- Serious health issues, such as anorexia.
- Indications of mental illness, such as severe depression or phobias.

## TEACHING AND TRAINING

Teaching and training are similar in that the teacher or trainer is seen as the expert sharing their knowledge and/or skills with the individuals they are instructing. The methods of teaching and training vary and, at best, are interactive and participative, giving those under instruction the chance to practise.

Many of the skills used in teaching and training can be employed when coaching. Teachers and managers find that coaching comes relatively easily to them as they are used to dealing with people in a variety of situations. The only difficulty is, as they put it, 'Taking off their own knowledge hats' or 'Stopping themselves from trying to fix it for people'.

## CONSULTANTS

A consultant is called in when you need expert advice and guidance in a field where you have little or no knowledge. A business consultant will be experienced and knowledgeable in a variety of areas that may include, among others:

- setting up systems and processes;
- information technology and data protection;
- finance and financial systems;
- employment law and legislation.

A consultant will share expertise, instruct managers and staff and visit regularly over a set period of time in order to support the implementation of any of the above.

## WHY IS COACHING SO VALUABLE?

Coaching is widely recognised as being of value and importance to most organisations. At its best it recognises and encourages every individual's growth and potential. It provides a safe space where individuals can explore areas that may otherwise remain just out of reach. Coaching supplies the challenge and support people need to face up to and to explore their undiscovered potential (see Figure 1).

**The coaching set-up**                    **The coaching partnership**

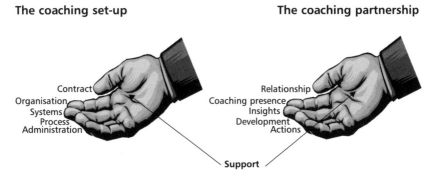

Contract
Organisation
Systems
Process
Administration

Relationship
Coaching presence
Insights
Development
Actions

Support

**Fig. 1. Coaching as support**

❝ *One doesn't discover new lands without consenting to lose sight of the shore for a very long time.* ❞

(André Gide)

Coaching enables people to discover their strengths, to concentrate on areas for development and to learn from their mistakes. It motivates them to move forward in their role, and to take responsibility for their goals and actions. It discourages the command and control method of management and, instead, nurtures and draws out each individual's hidden talent and skills.

Perhaps you can remember a time when you were involved in some kind of activity that stretched you beyond your own limits. You may have achieved something that at first appeared impossible. At school you may recall having a teacher who encouraged you to learn and pass an exam, despite feeling that you would surely fail. To be an effective coach, it is essential to believe in the potential of your staff allowing individuals to be heard and appreciated. This will have an amazing impact on their self-esteem and, ultimately, on their personal growth and job performance.

❝ *Coaching is an activity designed to improve performance . . . and coaching in the work place must involve turning work situations into learning opportunities as this is increasingly seen as an important part of what it is to manage.* ❞

(John Whitmore in Brealey, 2002)

❝ *[Coaching involves] developing a person's skills and knowledge so that their job performance improves, hopefully leading to achievement of organisational objectives. It targets high performance and improvement at work, although it may have an impact on an individual's private life. It usually lasts for a short period and focuses on skills and goals'.*

(Jarvis *et al.*, 2006)

Coaching skills can also be used to introduce a more collaborative approach to:

- appraisals;
- performance management;
- action learning; and
- meetings and group discussions.

A real advantage of coaching is that it encourages a person to focus on their strengths as well as areas for development. It enables individuals to challenge beliefs about themselves that may be holding them back. It can open a closed door and can release people from self-imposed restrictions. It gives people the permission to move forward in the way that is right for them.

Coaching is of value, therefore, because it promotes:

- increased confidence and self-awareness;
- enhanced emotional intelligence;
- effective resolution to issues and challenges;
- business/personal growth and career advancement;
- better decision-making and clarity around goals;
- improved time and stress management; and
- enhanced verbal and non-verbal communication skills (adapted from Association for Coaching, 2006).

## THE BENEFITS OF COACHING: SOME EXAMPLES

In 1999, as an ex-BBC radio broadcaster, I was asked to coach programme presenters at the BBC for them to gain confidence when tendering for new programme slots. The then Director General, Greg Dyke, was very open to creating a coaching culture. His vision was to 'make the BBC the most creative organisation in the world'. Today the BBC has forward-thinking leaders who have embraced and spread a culture of coaching throughout the organisation (see Chapter 17).

This has had a very positive effect on the way the BBC has handled the changes that have taken place within the organisation. Their leadership coaches have regular coaching supervision and have learnt to work more collaboratively. This has promoted an atmosphere of trust and openness among the staff and a willingness to learn from their mistakes. One-to-one coaching sessions and group coaching are carried out on a regular basis, thus helping staff to feel supported and valued.

Another example of where coaching has had an impact is a special needs school in London, where a coaching culture has been adopted by training senior staff to be workplace coaches. All professional conversations now take on a supportive coaching style, and one-to-one confidential coaching sessions have been set up for all who request them. As a result, the staff feel supported and this has increased motivation. This atmosphere of openness and trust extends to the classroom and meetings with parents, and it has had an immense impact on teaching and learning within the school.

Mentoring has also been a vital part of the programme as teachers new to their roles have benefited from having the advice and experience of more senior staff. Within two years, the school has gone from floundering at the bottom of the league tables to becoming a high-performing institution.

During the one-to-one voluntary coaching sessions, the following areas were identified as being particularly suited to coaching:

- Supporting and motivating staff.
- Staff setting and achieving their own development goals.
- Performance appraisals.
- Planning and structuring lessons.
- Professional coaching conversations following classroom observation.
- Solving problems.
- Communicating with colleagues and parents.
- Effective delegation.

> *The voyage of discovery is not in seeking new landscapes, but in having new eyes.*

(Marcel Proust)

At Upstream Connections (a web-design and optimisation company in Sussex), coaching sessions from an external coach were set up. This was initially for the four department managers on a regular fortnightly basis over 12 months. The main focus of the coaching was to support the newly-promoted managers in their roles. After the coaching programme, the managers identified the following as particularly useful:

- Developing themselves as managers through the one-to-one sessions.
- Unlocking areas of expertise and enhancing existing skills.

- The importance of effective delegation.
- Improved communication between individuals and departments.
- Feeling valued and supported.

As a result, the company has encouraged members of staff to adopt a coaching style of management. It feels this will result in more effective meetings, more motivated staff and enhanced performance. It also realised that its staff turnover was greatly reduced when people felt valued and supported. It has saved considerably on recruitment costs, and staff have taken charge of their own learning and development as a result of the coaching.

To become an effective coach, therefore, requires a great many skills, not least of which are the skills of an effective leader.

# 2

# Becoming an effective leader and coach

## WHAT MAKES A GOOD LEADER?

Think of someone who has been a leader for you in your life. This may have been a teacher, parent or grandparent, or a manager or boss:

- What behaviours did/do they exhibit that inspired you?
- Why are they important to you?

Some of the *behaviours* you thought of may be as follows. They:

- listened well;
- took time to understand your point of view;
- were non-judgemental;
- gave unconditional praise;
- allowed you space to grow and make mistakes;
- gave freely of their knowledge and wisdom;
- made you feel worthy and valued.

Today we call this using EI – emotional intelligence.

What comes to mind when you think of a great leader – what is it that makes them stand out, that makes them *important*? You may have identified their passion, energy, a certain presence, humour, humility and so on. These traits are about the way people come across: the qualities they show to the world.

Now think of someone who is slightly threatening to you. What do they do that causes this threat? Very often, someone appears threatening because they have not asked for permission before making a suggestion or request. They may use a question such as 'Why don't you do X?', which seems lightly accusing in tone.

A true leader, on the other hand, would show more humility by suggesting, 'Perhaps you would like to try X' This is more like an offer – you are free to make a choice. Obviously if you work in a position where 'orders' are vital, such as the fire service or army, then this approach would not always be advisable. However, people still feel resentful when they are not consulted – when they are not asked for their permission – and this can cause resistance.

## GIVING PERMISSION

When we ask people for their permission we are giving their power back to them, their sense of self-worth. We are validating them and their opinions – showing them that what they say/think/feel is of value. Good leaders know how to engage with people, and they create strong communities. Asking for permission also creates good boundaries. If you ask people for their permission, you get their buy-in and so there is no comeback later on. For example, you would invite a positive response if you said either of the following:

- Would you agree to meet out of your office for the coaching sessions as this would enable us to speak freely and would be less stressful?

- As your coach, I would like to suggest we have the sessions outside the office, as this can be more effective. Are you OK with that?

If, on the other hand, you said, 'I want us to have the sessions outside the office as this is more effective', you would not allow the person any choice and would end up inviting resentment and resistance.

You may be able to think of a few situations in your own job where asking permission could be useful. Think of a person you really trust: there may be no need for permission as the trust is inherent in the relationship. But everyone needs to feel valued and, even when you know that permission is not needed, rather than just taking it for granted, asking for permission can build on the trust you already have in place.

## WHAT IS THE INTENTION?

The *intention* behind the words is always more important than the words themselves. For example, in a meeting someone may say, 'Can I just finish!' Here the intention is: 'Shut up, I am speaking'. Or someone may say, 'I'm sure you don't mind my leaving early, do you?' The intention here is clearly 'I know this will not be convenient for you but I'm going anyway'.

## BEING A ROLE MODEL

As a leader, you will be aiming to be a role model: you will be someone who inspires others to be proud of their achievements, someone who guides and supports people so that they enjoy the journey as well as the end goal. Martin Luther King was a leader who inspired me as a young woman, and I, like many others, have never forgotten his 'I have a dream' speech. As I listened to that speech I had no inkling that one day, I would witness Barack Obama being elected as the first black president of the USA.

Martin Luther King spoke from the heart: he was totally authentic and it is this quality that marks a true leader. People will be looking to you as a leader of your department or organisation, to make authentic connections – to foster strong relationships so that people feel trusted and valued and are able to share their own vulnerability. As a leader in a coaching role, you will stand back from issues to see the bigger picture. You will be that person who is slightly in the background but whom everyone is aware of; a person with solid principles, a clear vision and shared purpose.

A leader, therefore, is someone who:

- can be trusted and who inspires trust;
- is consistent in dealing with people;
- supports mistakes;
- motivates others;
- takes time to listen;
- gives unconditional praise;
- has a vision and can communicate this vision;
- is able to delegate effectively;
- is influential;
- can manage expectations and disappointments;
- can justify decisions; and
- is proactive and energises others.

## Sharing leadership

In their book, *Power up: Transforming Organisations through Shared Leadership* (1998), David Bradford and Allan Cohen argue that a new model of shared leadership has become essential in today's markets:

❝ *In assuming overall responsibility for the results of their units, leaders over-manage their subordinates. When issues are discussed the topics are carefully restricted; the leader consults with subordinates when it seems appropriate but has the last say on critical decisions. This causes the subordinates to constrict their focus to their own areas, blame others, pass responsibility up to the boss and protect their flanks. Observing this the leader thinks "Just as I expected, those people cannot accept responsibility or do more than stick to their own assignments."* ❞

Observations such as this result in still greater control, which creates even more passivity among the employees. 'The boss doesn't want us to take responsibility', the employees conclude, 'so we'll only do what we're told.'

Shared leadership approaches do not undermine the leader's role or lead to the abandonment of hierarchy. As a leader, you still remain accountable for your group's performance and you will still need to make many final decisions. But you and your employees now need to collaborate more openly and frequently. This is where the coaching model can help to foster a more consultative and open approach to leadership.

## RECOGNISING INDIVIDUAL NEEDS

People do not have the same needs. Not all individuals, for example, want to be leaders. As a leader, you need to spot and support those individuals who have great skills, a sound work ethic, and the abilities to accept and solve problems, yet who do not have the desire to take on a leadership role. Being able to recognise when and where training is necessary, and guiding people to enhance their own personal growth, is, therefore, all part of good leadership.

## WHAT MAKES AN OUTSTANDING LEADER?

As well as the qualities listed earlier in this chapter, outstanding leaders also have the following in common:

- **Passion**: a love of what they do and the ability to put this over.
- **Courage**: they 'feel the fear and do it anyway'.
- **Humility**: they know that they are only as good as their own people.
- **Perseverance**: where there's a will there's a way.
- **Compassion**: they treat others with respect and kindness.
- **Forgiveness**: they forgive and allow people to learn by their mistakes.
- **Patience**: both with themselves and with others.
- **Strong values**: authentic, trustworthy, honest, reliable, committed, consultative and loyal.

The following are a few of the skills good leaders possess and the results of their practising these skills.

- **Effective communication** results in positive action.
- **Valuing people** results in increased motivation.
- **Listening deeply** results in people feeling they are being heard and that their opinions matter.

Perhaps you would like to add to this list.

## MANAGERS/COACHES

Managers may find it difficult to adjust to being a coach. People look to managers for guidance and so managers often find it unnatural to listen and not to give advice and suggestions. A good manager/coach, however, is someone who:

■ is approachable;
■ can be strategic;
■ is a good listener;
■ keeps an eye on targets/results;
■ is consistent;
■ is open to suggestions;
■ can be flexible while keeping boundaries;
■ is inspiring;
■ makes people feel valued and supported;
■ allows people the freedom to grow in their role;
■ supports mistakes; and
■ is encouraging and positive;

A manager is the person to whom people look for actions and decisions. They are the vital link to the leadership team and essential to the organisation's purpose. They are responsible for keeping the ship on an even keel and for balancing their commitments to their team with those of the organisation.

# 3

# Internal and external coaching

When you work as an *external* coach, you tend to work in isolation. You can arrange coaching via telephone sessions for an agreed period of time or arrange face-to-face meetings with your coachee. The venue may be your place of work or that of your coachee. An external coach has no hidden agenda and no vested interest in the outcome of the sessions. Naturally, an external coach wants their coachee to be satisfied and to achieve their goals, but an external coach is not there to influence their coachee's final decisions – indeed, it is desirable that the coach should be as unattached to the outcome as possible. The sessions are led by the coachee, and the coach is there to be a mirrored sounding board. The coach will encourage their coachee to set goals and, when appropriate, will challenge certain beliefs and behaviours that may be holding their coachee back from achieving these goals.

As an external coach, you will not be involved in the coachee's decisions that may affect others in the workplace. An external coach is not guided by what may have happened before in the organisation or what will happen in the future. They are totally objective and removed from workplace relationships and company culture.

An *internal* coach, on the other hand, carries a good deal of organisational baggage. They are involved with various relation-

ships and understand the organisation's cu|
the day-to-day communication systems and v
will take on other responsibilities that may coi
as a coach. These roles may include mentoi
appraisals and handling discipline problems.

The manager as coach will have information about a member of staff that will, potentially, influence the interventions made during the coaching sessions. Coaching supervision is, therefore, highly recommended to ensure safety, trust and ongoing development (see Chapter 15).

## CREATING A PARTNERSHIP OF EQUALS

Ideally, the coaching partnership is of two equals working alongside each other: where the individual feels really heard and respected. As an internal coach, the power difference between you – as a leader – and your staff could be a barrier to the effectiveness of the coaching. In order for coaching to be effective and lasting, you should create a space of shared intimacy and acceptance. This may be difficult to achieve when you are coaching and/or line managing someone whom you find difficult to respect. This was the situation when I was once supervising Judy, a newly-qualified internal coach.

### Case study

*Judy had been line managing a member of staff for three years and thus knew him well. She did not think he was a particularly effective member of the team and had found herself making judgements about how effective the coaching would be: "He never listens to advice and has always been reluctant to change. I cannot see how coaching will turn that around".*

*er I had asked her if he had any talents or particular skills she had noticed, Judy was able to list several of his strengths. She realised that, by thinking of her colleague in a positive light, she would bring a different energy to the session. She realised how important it was to empty her head of previous knowledge and assumptions. That way the coaching session would have a positive focus and more chance of success.*

The next case study reports the observations of a manager who, at first, wasn't sure of the outcome of the coaching.

### Case study

*'I discovered that my perception of the team member I coached was different from her revealed self and this helped me align future expectations, and made me much more aware of where her energies and skills could be best used. The exploratory nature of coaching brightened her self-awareness and confidence. In addition it helped her develop in her role as she became more conscious of her achievements and aspirations.*

*'The arrangement relied heavily on trust as a fundamental base. My colleague was able to expose herself to the process, as she knew I would treat information and insights with professionalism and confidentiality, as established in our contract. Our relationship went up a gear too as a respectful bond became a by-product of the experience'* (contributed by Helen Bale, a corporate health and safety manager).

## FINDING SOLUTIONS

As a manager or team leader, you may be supporting your team as a mentor. This may include giving advice, sharing your knowledge and answering questions to enable individuals to progress. In a coaching role, you will achieve more lasting results if you put all the advice and expertise to one side and allow the coachee to find their own answers and solutions. This is not easy when you have been in the position of your staff's 'solution finder'. In addition, people will need to be informed about your change of style. If they are used to getting answers from you, they may feel let down when none are forthcoming.

Sam Sheppard is a newly trained Institute of Leadership and Management (ILM) management coach working for Kent County Council. As a line manager she was hesitant about coaching in case she began to influence the outcome of the sessions:

❝ *My belief that everyone is capable of change has helped me be patient with coachees that have been slow to recognise solutions to issues that I feel are quite obvious. I think that this belief has helped to counterbalance my impatience with people who are capable of doing things, but choose not to.*

*Of my three coachees I work with two of them. I was initially a bit worried about how I would manage this but my ability to establish and maintain appropriate professional and personal boundaries has helped greatly. One of my coachees gave me the following feedback which supports this: "Sam let me control the way that we worked – putting the onus back on me to think through situations rather than giving me the answers."*

*And another wrote: "It must have been hard for you to keep that distance, allowing me to speak about issues I know you also experience and have opinions about. You're totally professional."* ❞

These insights illustrate how, even when you think you know what is going on in your coachee's mind, it is vital to put aside this knowledge and to work with what comes up in the sessions. Your coachees may be underperforming and not working to their full potential. You may have clear ideas about how they could change and what actions they need to take. Allowing them space to explore what is holding them back and your belief in their ability to identify appropriate actions can have a huge impact on their self-esteem and overall performance. Furthermore, a solution that was successful for you may not be appropriate for your coachee, as the following case study shows.

## Case study

*A headteacher (Annette) was coaching a member of staff (Julie) who had come up with a solution to encourage the quieter members of her class. The head confided in me as her supervisor that she felt this solution was, in her words 'A bit off the wall', and that she was very reluctant to allow Julie to try out her idea. Annette was encouraged to talk it over with Julie in her coaching session to get a better picture of how the solution might work. Annette was encouraged to look for the possible advantages and to let Julie give it a try.*

The following are a couple of questions from the coaching session:

*Annette*: Julie, tell me a bit more about how you feel this solution would work. (*Julie explained this.*) Yes, I see. I have a clearer picture of how this could work now. Is there anything else you need to think of?

This last question allows Julie to reflect. It shows that the coach trusts the process and gives Julie time to expand her thinking. In this way she is able to explore her idea while, at the same time, feeling supported. This is very motivating and can unlock the coachee's creative side.

Annette was pleasantly surprised at the results. Although she would not have approached this problem in the same way, she realised that Julie's personality had affected the outcome. Annette understood that giving Julie the freedom to try out her ideas had also boosted her confidence.

## Avoiding the pitfalls of internal coaching

Apart from finding solutions for your coachee, there are other pitfalls an internal coach can easily fall into.

### Leading the coachee to a solution

Try not to 'lead' your coachee to an obvious solution to the problem. For example:

*Coach*: So presenting these results to the board on Friday is not what you want to do?

*Coachee*: No, I just don't feel ready.

*Coach*: Umm. What about asking Bob to help you? He's great at presenting. (*Jumping to a solution.*)

*Coachee*: Well, it's not really the presentation skills I'm concerned about. I just feel I need more time to prepare.

A more useful exchange here would have been as follows:

*Coachee*: I just don't feel ready.

*Coach*: What would you need to feel 'ready'? (*Using the coachee's language*)

*Coachee*: Well, I would need to prepare all the PowerPoint slides and make sure I had all the figures clear in my head.

*Coach*: How long would that take you?

*Coachee*: Well, I could ask someone in Communications to sort out the PowerPoint I suppose. Perhaps it's just the figures I need to go through myself. Umm. I've got till the end of the week.

*Coach*: So where does that leave you?

*Coachee*: Actually, Friday looks manageable when I think about it.

By coming out of 'fix it' mode the coach has allowed the coachee to come to their own solution. In the first exchange the coach had assumed it was the lack of presentation skills that was holding the coachee back and had jumped in with their own idea. Staying back and supporting the coachee while they thought things through enabled the coachee to come up with a solution that was best *for them*.

## Showing your judgement non-verbally

Try to remain curious without showing judgement in the tone of your voice, facial expressions or body language:

*Coach*: This issue of *x* is something that seems to be hovering in the background. I am wondering if it has any significance here? (*Relaxed, neutral tone of voice.*)

*Coach*: I am sensing a reluctance to take this further. Is there anything more that needs to be considered here?

Be curious and keep your voice neutral and even. This part of the session may be a difficult area for the coachee to delve into. Be respectful and allow the coachee to consider their reply. If there is the slightest hint of judgement, the session will close down.

## Wanting your staff to succeed

Try not to become over-enthusiastic about your coachee's development. As a manager or leader, you will want your staff to perform well. Your staff may be highly motivated and may appear to be on top of things. As their coach, you could be pulled along by their commitment and energy. If you are, you are in danger of allowing your staff to fail or to promise more than they can deliver.

Staff often want to please their manager or coach, and, as a result, they may sometimes make decisions or commitments they find hard to keep. As a coach, you will need to check how realistic their goals are. Ensure your staff are well equipped to tackle the tasks they have set for themselves:

*Coach*: So you think you will be ready for this presentation on Friday?

*Coachee*: Yes, that seems possible now.

*Coach*: Good. So what exactly is your plan of action now?

*Coachee*: Well, I need to go over the data and decide how many PowerPoint slides I need and roughly design them. Then contact Peter in comms to see if he is willing to set them up for me. Oh, and I need to take some time to go through them and make some adjustments.

*Coach*: Is that all possible before Friday?

*Coachee*: Actually, that seems like a rush. I think that I would feel better about presenting it next week and getting it right. It would give everyone more time and I would feel calmer about it.

Once again, this allows the coachee to reach a decision that is right for them – it is not setting them up to fail.

## Pushing for a result

There will be times when, as a coach, you will be frustrated by the lack of progress in a coaching session, and you may thus be tempted to push your coachee to get a result. In many companies there is a time pressure to get things completed. If at all possible, avoid rushing your coachees. Some people thrive under pressure and love to be challenged. Others need the time with you to reflect on decisions and may even need to go away from the workplace to consider the ideas they have brought up in the session. If they are given this time they will trust the process, and their decision-making will become more confident as a result.

❝ *Why endeavour to straighten the road of life? The faster we travel the less there is to see.* ❞

(Helen Hayes)

## Making assumptions

Try not to make assumptions about your coachee based on your previous experience of them or on the way they have performed in the past.

### Case study

*Jenny, a member of the leadership team, had been asked to coach a colleague she felt was not pulling her weight. Jenny's initial reaction was to decline, but she decided to go ahead and to see what transpired. She had been encouraged by her coach supervisor to go into the session with a clean slate and no judgement as to the outcome of the sessions.*

*At the first meeting Jenny explained clearly that she was acting as coach and that this relationship was one of equality. Jenny presented her coachee with documents explaining the process and the agreed timings and boundaries.*

*After three coaching sessions Jenny arrived at her coaching supervision with the following comments:*

*'At first I was sceptical as to the success of the coaching sessions. I had definite opinions about this colleague and felt that she had not been particularly effective. After taking stock and putting my preconceptions to one side I entered into the sessions with as little judgement as possible. I allowed myself to focus on the potential of my coachee and a few of the strengths I knew she had. I was surprised at the outcome. There was far more background to the issues of "under achievement" than I had realised. This coachee had not had sufficient training in the areas she was expected to work in and this had not come to my attention in her appraisals. I was amazed at the efficient way she had managed a couple of projects that I had also not been aware of.*

*I would say that coaching supported and encouraged this coachee to be far more open and honest with me. After three months I came to respect her in a way that would not otherwise have been possible. I also learnt a great deal about myself and the assumptions I had been making.'*

# 4

# The differences between coaching and mentoring

You do not need to be in coaching mode all the time – there will always be occasions when new staff or less experienced individuals need mentoring. Such people would become very frustrated if you withheld your knowledge and expertise at all times. You will, therefore, at times, need to draw on your knowledge to guide and support your staff.

In a mentoring role, you will be guiding people to make the best decisions both for them *and* for the organisation. One suggestion is that, at the end of a *coaching* session, you ask, 'I have some advice and experience that may help you. Would you like to hear my ideas?' This way the coaching session can remain 'advice free' and the coachee has the opportunity to accept or decline the advice or ideas. There may also be occasions when, if you feel the individual is in danger of harming themselves or others by their actions or that a course of action will jeopardise the organisation, you will need to advise against it. Hopefully, this will rarely occur.

## DISTINGUISHING BETWEEN COACHING AND MENTORING

Table 1 lists some distinctions between coaching and mentoring, although many of these roles naturally can, and do, overlap.

Table 1   The differences between coaching and mentoring

| A coach... | A mentor... |
| --- | --- |
| Creates space to think | Advises and suggests |
| Is non-judgemental | May need to make judgements |
| Gives ownership | Leads by example |
| Challenges | Helps to develop |
| Need not be an expert | Is usually more experienced |
| Stands back | Stands close |
| Gives responsibility back | Can feel responsible |
| Challenges beliefs, thoughts and behaviours | Shares knowledge and experience |
| Asks 'What decision?' | Guides to a decision |
| Draws out examples and ideas | Gives examples and ideas |
| Works within a set time frame | May work over a long period |
| Focuses on specific development areas | Takes a broader view |

While the most rewarding outcomes from both coaching and mentoring will be realised in a structured, confidential, one-to-one session, this does not mean you will never coach or mentor in a snatched moment in the corridor or lift. If a member of staff asks a brief question, as a mentor you can give them an answer that will act as a quick fix (see also 'Coaching on the spot' below).

## KNOWING WHEN TO COACH AND WHEN TO MENTOR

There will be opportunities both to coach and to mentor throughout the day. The key is to be sure of which technique you are using and of the rationale behind it. For example, as a *mentor* with more expertise than your mentee:

*Gill*: Oh, Mr Adams, can you give me the initial steps when setting up the database for the online client accounts?

*Mr A*: Yes, of course. I'll email a few bullet points when I'm back at my desk in a couple of minutes.

*Gill*: Great, thanks.

As a *coach* it is useful to have brief coaching exchanges to foster responsibility in your coachees:

*Gill*: Mr Adams, I have set up the database but am not sure how to gather all the information on the various clients. Can you help?

*Mr A*: Yes. Have you got any idea where this information may be stored?

*Gill*: Well, I guess Jim may have the client details as he set this up initially on the old system. I could certainly ask him.

*Mr A*: Yes, that sounds like a good idea. Anything else that occurs to you?

*Gill*: Yes, the new clients' details are stored automatically as they log on to the system so I could ask Emma if she can transfer them over.

*Mr A*: Excellent. That seems to be settled, then.

Of course, Mr Adams could have easily given all this information to Gill. By using the skills of questioning and listening to her needs, he has enabled her to find her own answers. How much more motivating is this for your staff? It also has the added bonus that, once people gain confidence, they will not keep bothering you with questions; it encourages them to think things through for themselves.

Very understandably, people who have received mentoring in the past tend to go back for further help. This may be appropriate but, as a leader, you perhaps want to encourage them to think things through before asking you for guidance. Coaching would help here. Through coaching, staff gain confidence and increase their knowledge.

As a leader, you may find that your staff become more independent and begin to make their own decisions. This will free you up to carry out your own role more effectively. You will need to select instinctively whether to use coaching or mentoring in such a situation. New staff and those new to a role will, for example, in the first instance need mentoring. Once they become more experienced, however, coaching may be the more appropriate method to encourage self-development.

## COACHING 'ON THE SPOT'

Coaching on the spot is a supportive conversation rather than a 'telling' one. It involves using some of the skills of coaching that all good managers already know:

- Listening without judgement.
- Staying with the person while they explain their needs.
- Giving eye contact and full attention to the situation.
- Allowing your questions to draw out the knowledge from the individual.
- Supporting them to come to a decision.
- Tapping in to their own knowledge and skills.

Coaching does not always need a formal structure to be effective. It does, however, need trust, patience, skilled questions, sensitivity and the ability to create rapport. Above all, it requires you to believe that your member of staff knows the answer. It requires you to put aside your need to 'fix it' for them: to allow them to own the task or find the solution that is best for *them*.

## COACHING IS A TWO-WAY PROCESS

You should bear in mind that the relationship between you and your employees is the key to the success of coaching. Staying focused on them and allowing them time to think things through are vital to the results.

> ❛ *The quality of your listening will establish the quality of their thinking.* ❜

(Klein, 1999)

You may encounter resistance and challenges from your coachees, and they may cause you to rethink areas of your own role. When you begin coaching, one of the great by-products is your own self-development. If you are willing learn from your staff and to accept that some changes in your own behaviour may be necessary, then your coaching will achieve greater acceptance.

## ESTABLISHING THE DIFFERENCES BETWEEN COACHING AND MENTORING

You should have a clear definition of what coaching is and be able to clarify the differences between coaching and mentoring. This ensures that the boundaries around giving advice and suggestions are clear and that coaching does not become confused with mentoring. Both disciplines are of value, but need to be treated as separate methods of developing people.

It is useful in a session to make the coachee aware of the times when you are coaching. The session will be more productive if you manage to make this clear. Advice and suggestions (mentoring) may be offered at the end of the session. For example:

*Coach*: I have some knowledge of this subject and would like to offer a suggestion. Would you like to hear it?

*Coachee*: Yes please. (*Or they may prefer to go away and try out their own idea first.*)

As long as the offer is made in this way it will not intrude on the growth and self-esteem of the individual being coached.

# 5

# Establishing the right climate

When you set up one-to-one or group coaching and mentoring sessions, it is vital to establish a climate that encourages and supports risk-taking. People need to feel safe in order to divulge information and to share ideas. It is also vital that all the stakeholders subscribe to the process and are totally committed to the programme.

Everyone should, therefore, be clear about the following:

- What coaching is and what it isn't (for the differences between coaching, mentoring, counselling and consulting, see Chapter 1).
- Why coaching is being introduced (what it will support/ influence/change).
- How it will be carried out (one to one, group, peer, face to face, over the telephone).
- What it will address (overarching values, goals, outcomes).

To achieve a climate in which coaching will be effective, therefore, you should ensure that the sessions are:

- well organised and confidential;
- non-judgemental;
- objective;
- respectful;

- challenging;
- manageable;
- time bound;
- quiet and uninterrupted;
- focused on the coachee's best interests; and
- operating within legal and ethical parameters.

## WELL ORGANISED AND CONFIDENTIAL

Developing a clear flexible plan is essential, with the lead practitioner establishing the goals for the programme and how these will link to the organisation's vision. The roles and responsibilities of all the stakeholders should be discussed and clear time frames established. Contractual agreements should be drawn up that make provision for who will be coached, how the coaches will be chosen and how the results of the coaching or mentoring will be assessed and evaluated. These agreements must also make provision for the confidentiality of the sessions.

The nature and frequency of the sessions should also be agreed, and effective record-keeping systems put in place to enable continuous improvement and monitoring. If codes of practice for coaching sessions are drawn up, these should clarify expectations, set the boundaries and emphasise the need for confidentiality. There will usually be a mid-session and a final review to evaluate the outcomes against the sessions' goals and objectives.

## BEING NON-JUDGEMENTAL

It is never easy when you are coaching internally to be totally non-judgemental. However, if you put aside your own knowledge and experience of the coachee and start with a clean slate, you will stimulate faster growth.

Before each coaching session, allow yourself time to do the following:

## Exercise

- *Sit yourself comfortably in the room allocated.*
- *Visualise the coachee and all you know about them.*
- *Now allow your knowledge and beliefs about them to fade away into the distance. Imagine this knowledge floating out of the window so that they are no longer a part of who the coachee is.*
- *Next, imagine this individual as someone with great potential and hidden talents yet to be discovered.*

*If you are able to bring these positive thoughts and energy your the coaching sessions, you may be surprised at the results.*

## Case study

*In a financial organisation in Sussex, one of the senior managers was considered 'difficult'. He was set in his ways and people found him to be abrasive. He was, in their opinion, not able to 'deal with people effectively'.*

*After coaching him for a number of sessions, it was apparent that his abrasive attitude was very much a reaction to how he was perceived: 'Well, if people see me as abrasive, then that's probably how I am.' After discussing this with his boss he was able to explain that, if they would begin to see him as someone who had the potential to change, his own behaviour may become less abrasive. The outcome was that, through coaching, this manager was able to work on his people skills. With the support he received from his colleagues, he was allowed to 'see' himself in a different light.*

When we see the potential in others and support them to find solutions that are obscured by limiting beliefs, we may light a flame that has long been extinguished.

## ENSURING OBJECTIVITY

You would be advised to bring objectivity to the sessions but, as the case study above shows, this can be a challenge when you work as an internal coach. It is important that you remain neutral and are able to mirror your coachee's thoughts and ideas. We all come to coaching with our own world-view and our own filters. At least if we are aware of this we can pay careful attention to the times when we may intrude on our coachee's world. The action and agreements made by the coachee need to be owned by the coachee – they will not be as effective if they have been influenced by the coach.

## REMAINING RESPECTFUL

We all have attitudes, beliefs and values that shape the way we think and behave. No one person's view is necessarily wrong or right (unless it breaks the law or an organisation's codes and ethics). It is the coach's role, therefore, to respect – while not necessarily agreeing with – the attitudes, values and beliefs held by their coachee. If we are disrespectful of another's view, we relinquish our own spiritual intelligence.

## BEING CHALLENGING

Individuals often come to coaching because they want to be challenged. They enjoy the way a coach enables them to think sideways: holds a mirror up and encourages creative thought.

People often, however, bring negative beliefs and assumptions about themselves to sessions, and it is the coach's role to challenge these beliefs while also remaining respectful.

Negative beliefs are sometimes generalisations:

1. 'I will never be able to achieve this goal. I haven't the skills.'

2. 'I am always late for appointments.'

3. 'They always set impossible targets.'

Gentle probing will often reveal fears or concerns around the goal or skills being described. The following are a few questions to use for statements 1–3 above:

1. 'Never? What if you did have the skills?' Or 'Never? What would need to change for you to achieve this goal?'

2. When have you ever been early? Or 'What appointments do you arrive on time for?' Or 'What do you need to change so you can arrive early?' Or 'What would be the benefits for you of arriving early?'

3. What makes the targets impossible?' Or 'What targets have you reached?' Or 'What would need to happen for these targets to be met?' Or 'What would make these targets possible?'

See Chapter 7 for an exercise on challenging limiting beliefs.

## Case study

*The chief executive of an international company in Switzerland told me it was impossible for him not to take work home at night. His home life was suffering, but he was convinced that his productivity would also suffer if he left his laptop at work. After challenging his assumption and asking him, 'What needs to happen for you to be able to leave your briefcase at work?' he replied,*

*'Well, I'd have to be more organised with my time.'*

*On further exploration he was able to see that he often wasted precious time. He realised that, if he was able to work more productively, he could leave his laptop behind. He had got into a habit of taking work home and was convinced this was necessary. It only took a couple of weeks for him to realise that it was just that – a habit. Thinking creatively, he was able to save time and to spend quality time with his family.*

## ENSURING MANAGEABILITY

It is important that the coachee creates a plan with results that are attainable, measurable and specific. The coachee will be encouraged by their coach to set target dates for any goals they have identified. These goals should stretch the coachee while, at the same time, being realistic.

While there *is* generally a specific goal people are working towards, it is useful for coachees to explore options and to be encouraged to think creatively. As a coach, use your own judgement as to how much time people need to reach a specific, manageable goal.

## TIME-BOUND

Manageable and time-bound are linked. People often come to coaching with unrealistic expectations or very long-term goals. They may be seeking promotion where there are clearly no possibilities or they may want a senior management position but are not ready to take that step. It is up to the coach to encourage and, at the same time, to help them to be realistic. If goals are not manageable or realistic, then you are setting them up to fail.

Long-term goals can be broken down into sizeable chunks. The coachee can be encouraged to plan the stages in the process, with small achievable goals along the way. As far as possible, they should be able to set their own deadlines and time frames to suit themselves. This way they will take more responsibility for the outcomes.

## QUIET AND UNINTERRUPTED

Creating a quiet space for the sessions to take place will enhance the quality of the session. If you are line managing someone you coach, it is not advisable to have the coaching sessions in your office. It is generally far better to hold coaching sessions 'off site' if this can be arranged. However, in most companies this is not possible, so find a relaxing environment where you will not be interrupted. It cannot be stressed enough how much the environment has an impact on the successful outcome of the sessions.

## FOCUSING ON YOUR COACHEE'S BEST INTERESTS

When coaching internally, there will always be an agenda that has been set by the organisation. There may even be management or leadership behaviours that have been identified as desirable. There may also be set organisational goals that the sessions are directed towards. With this in mind, the sessions should always be conducted in the coachee's best interests. This does not mean that the organisation is compromised in any way – it just means that, if the individual is happy, then their work will improve and they will become more productive.

It is possible for the sessions to be focused on the coachee's thoughts, ideas and goals and yet still be of benefit to the organisation. For this to happen, all the stakeholders need to be aware that it is equally important to coach the person as well as the objectives.

## Case study

*In a city council planning office, ten managers were being coached. The council had realised that many staff had been off sick due to stress. They wanted to support their managers and help them to achieve a better work–life balance. They did not realise what an impact this would have on the working life of those individuals. Not only did they achieve a drastic reduction in stress-related absence but they also retained several staff who had been threatening to leave.*

*As a result of coaching, one member of staff did leave. This had been flagged up at the outset and, as a result, this member of staff was able to find a much more suitable position in another organisation. The council did not lose out as they realised they could promote another, more suitable member of staff to the vacant position. After the six months' coaching-programme evaluation, the improvement in targets being met by the department rose by 20%.*

## OPERATING WITHIN LEGAL AND ETHICAL PARAMETERS

It is vital that coaching programmes are operated within the legal and policy framework that underpins all employment relationships. This includes being aware of the following:

- The race, sex and disability discrimination Acts.
- Employment law, health and safety regulations, equality at work legislation, grievance procedures and the codes of conduct outlined in the organisation's policies and procedures.
- Issues of power and authority.
- Clearly established coaching boundaries.

(See the websites at the end of the book for the International Coach Federation, European Mentoring and Coaching Council and Association for Coaching ethics, standards and codes of practice.)

As a coach or mentor you would be advised to:

- be truthful and have integrity;
- build trust; and
- promote self-awareness.

## BEING TRUTHFUL AND HAVING INTEGRITY

You will have a gut feeling of what you consider to be right and what wrong: you will instinctively know when issues are uncomfortable. Coaching is, at its best, truthful and open. It is very liberating for your coachee to hear your truth and to know that they are dealing with a professional. There may be times, however, when you will not be able to put aside some sensitive knowledge or opinions you have formed. Despite your best efforts, a coachee may also continually step over the boundaries and make you feel vulnerable. In such situations it is necessary to state the truth, as you see it, as sensitively as you can.

## Case study

*Mary had been offered coaching as part of a promotional package that involved her taking a management role in the company. She had been very manipulative and had eased her way to this position by undermining a close colleague of her coach. The coach was not able to put this aside and asked the coaching programme co-ordinator to find her another coach. This was the right decision on the coach's behalf.*

# BUILDING TRUST

Coaching is built on strong foundations of trust. It is vital that managers or leaders can express what they are feeling. It can be very lonely at the top of any profession or organisation. There are few people to whom senior staff can turn for honest feedback. Not many people will challenge their decisions or question their judgement. The leader as coach can, and will, take up this mantle, but this can only occur if there is mutual trust and respect for the process.

Contracting is also important in building trust as this sets clear boundaries, agreements and measurements of success. It also allows all the stakeholders to be clear about the issues to be addressed and firms up confidentiality and reporting processes.

## PROMOTING SELF-AWARENESS

Not everyone's beliefs, attitudes and values align with your own. When you work as an internal coach, it will sometimes be necessary to keep in mind the organisation's values as well as your coachee's. By being respectful of others' views and beliefs, you will achieve a greater rapport with your coachees.

Using self-reflection also increases awareness and, as you mirror and sensitively question your coachees, they will begin to realise how their own behaviour may be affecting others.

Some questions you could ask in a *neutral curious tone* include the following:

- What effect do you think your intervention may have had?
- What was the reaction to your suggestion?
- How far do you think they understood your proposal?
- What impact did your remarks have on the team?
- If that was addressed to you, how would you react do you think?
- What could you have said differently in this situation?

The coach's own self-reflection is, naturally, an important part of this process (see Chapter 15).

# 6

# Coaching models

## DEVELOPING PEOPLE SKILLS

You may be coming to coaching from a specialist area, such as finance, engineering or IT, where your skills and knowledge have been valued. You may not have had the opportunity to develop your people skills and, when faced with coaching members of your team, you may feel this is a very daunting challenge. This is where a coaching model may be helpful.

A model is a predetermined method or procedure you can follow when coaching. While there are a variety of coaching models you can employ, not all coaching sessions will need a model. They can, however, be a useful focus for a session when a clear goal has been identified. Many coaches do not use models at all and, after coaching for several years, you will develop an instinct for what is needed. However, some coaches do prefer to work with a model, so it is up to you to be adaptable in your approach.

Coaching models are only useful if they serve a real purpose. People often come to a session in a reflective state of mind – they may want to explore certain strategies or rethink a project. Your role as their coach would be to act as a sounding board, showing curiosity and expanding their thinking. In such cases a model may not be appropriate.

## The **GROW** model

The most well-known coaching model is the GROW model. This is a management tool for problem-solving and development. It was originally created by Graham Alexander and was further developed by Sir John Whitmore. The idea behind this model is that you support people during their progress from identifying their goals to taking clear action.

GROW is an acronym for **G**oals (the exploration of), **R**eality (the current situation), **O**ptions (the opportunities available), **W**hat (a willingness to take action):

- **Goals**: identify the long or short-term objectives.
- **Reality**: explore the current situation and provide support to find the positive aspects.
- **Options**: discuss the choices, strategies and possibilities available.
- **What**: establish what will be done and when. Who will do it and by when? Is there the will to do it?

In coaching, this model is best used in a context of awareness and responsibility, with the aim of increasing these two key qualities, otherwise it is no more than a mechanical problem-solving tool and will not achieve optimum performance results. When taking your coachee through the above steps, it may become apparent that they have no specific goal, in which case 'reality' and 'options' may be better places to start.

The coach prepares the coachee by introducing the model and by showing them the process. The coach then asks open questions (see below) and uses other coaching methods discussed in this book to support the coachee to work through each phase.

While obtaining commitment may not always be appropriate, it is very useful to check how willing your coachee is to move forward and to take responsibility for their choices. Many coachees are also pleased to have some accountability for their actions. (We all need a nudge now and then!) A sheet of paper outlining the model can then be given to your coachee, or you can just talk your coachee through the model as a guide.

## ASKING OPEN QUESTIONS

Open questions are useful for both coaching and mentoring. Kipling wrote (*Just So Stories*, 1902):

> ❝ *I keep six honest serving men*
> *(They taught me all I knew);*
> *Their names are What and Why and When*
> *And How and Where and Who.* ❞

The following are a few open questions for you to add to, amend or change to suit your purpose:

- What would you like to use this session for?
- If you had an outcome for this session, what would that be?
- Anything else/what else? (Useful questions to repeat several times.)
- What could be done to move this forward?
- What's stopping you?
- How far is that true/is that a belief?
- If you were to do *x*, what would the consequences be? (Possibly the opposite of what they said.)
- What would that result in?

- How do you see your role in this?
- What needs to happen now?
- What one action would make a difference?
- What I heard you say was...is this correct?
- So what you mean is...is that correct?
- What resources/skills/people do you need?
- How can they/I support you?
- What have you already got in place?
- How can you find alternative ways to explore/use this information?
- What assumptions could you be making?
- In what way are these assumptions valid, relevant, true?
- What are the implications of this?
- Have you considered $x/y$?
- What needs to happen now?
- Would you agree that we've covered $x/y$?
- Are you happy to take this forward?
- What actions can you now commit to?
- Who else will you need to involve?
- When will you report back to me on this?
- How will you measure your success/results?
- On a scale of 1–10, how do you feel this session has worked for you?
- What would you like to focus on in the next session?

## THE ERR MODEL

If your coachee is suppressing their feelings and emotions, an atmosphere of trust that is so essential to growth will not be established. A model I have developed that can be used effectively when coachees are caught in the emotion of a situation is ERR.

This model was created to give focus to a session when emotions are running high (see Figure 2). ERR is an acronym for Emotion (acknowledge the feelings), **R**eality (focus on the reality/facts), **R**esponsibility (encourage responsibility and positive actions).

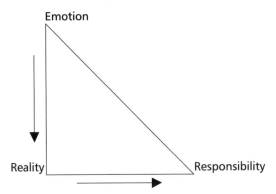

**Fig. 2. The ERR model.**

## Acknowledging the emotion

First, acknowledge the emotion. If you ask your coachee how they are managing a particular project and they respond, 'Oh, I am frankly frustrated and annoyed by the slow progress. It seems to be taking up so much of my time', you have several options:

- You could respond with a quick comment, such as, 'Well, I guess you'll find a way through'.
- You could act with more emotional intelligence and say, 'That's surprising. You usually manage to stay on top of things'.
- You could offer a really emotionally intelligent response, such as: 'Yes, I notice you are frustrated by the slow progress' (recognition and acknowledgement of the emotion). 'What, if anything, have you managed to do so far?' (moving the focus to the reality of what has been done).

If your coachee feels understood and the emotions are managed well, the session can continue.

*Note*: If your coachee is unable to proceed and the emotion is connected to areas you are not comfortable with, they may need to be referred to a counsellor.

## Recognising the reality

Once they have agreed to proceed, there are a variety of ways to continue. For example:

- What support do you need to take this forward?
- What are the facts of this situation? (Reflect the coachee's thoughts to them.)
- What exactly do you know? (Again, allow the coachee to hear what they said by reflecting key areas.)
- What specifically is the issue here? (Focus on the positive aspects, 'Yes, I see. How can you overcome this?')

## Taking responsibility

Below are some questions that may help your coachee to take responsibility for future action:

- What needs to happen now?
- What specifically do you want to do/happen?
- What support do you need?
- What actions will you now take?

Reflect or summarise for your coachee, and always believe they will find a solution. This gives the responsibility back to your coachee and allows them to feel heard and appreciated.

# Situation + Thoughts + Space + Reactions = Result

> ❝ *Between stimulus and response there is a space.*
> *In that space is the power to choose our response.*
> *In our response lies our growth and our freedom.* ❞

(Viktor Frankl)

As a coach, it is not always easy to stop to think about how to respond in a situation where emotions are running high. A model that can be employed in such situations is Situation + Thoughts + Reactions = Result. In this model, as Viktor Frankl suggests, it is Space that makes the difference:

- **Situation**: in a coaching session, your coachee offers a proposal for you to consider together.
- **Thoughts**: you think this proposal is a waste of time and you are not fully engaged.
- **Reaction**: your coachee appears hesitant and you are further frustrated by this.
- **Result**: when the session ends, your relationship with your coachee has suffered a real setback.

If, however, you had inserted a Space between your thoughts and your reaction, you may have decided to give the proposal a chance. You would have listened without judgement and, because of your reaction, your coachee would have been better able to explain their proposal. There may have been some good points you could have focused on and the result of the session would have been more positive for both parties: 'In our response lies our growth and our freedom'.

## THE JOHARI WINDOW

The Johari window was named after Joseph Luft and Harry Ingham and is a useful model to consider in coaching and mentoring as it shows human interaction (Luft, 1969). The Johari window four-quadrant model divides personal awareness into four distinct areas (see Figure 3) in which an individual is represented by their own window.

| | Known to self | Not known to self |
|---|---|---|
| Known to others | 1<br><br>OPEN | 2<br><br>BLIND |
| Not known to others | HIDDEN<br><br>3 | UNKNOWN<br><br>4 |

**Fig. 3. The Johari window.**

In relation to coaching, the first 'open' quadrant shows things the coachee knows about themselves (for example, who they are, what they do, where they live and so on). It can also include feelings and values. On first meeting, this window is small but enlarges as the individual gets to know the coach and shares information.

The second 'blind' quadrant shows things a person meeting the coachee knows about them but that the coachee is unaware of (for example, that they are using an incorrect term or word in their conversation, or that they have their jacket buttoned incorrectly).

The third 'hidden' quadrant shows things the coachee knows about themselves (for example, that they grew up in Ghana or that their favourite colour is green). When you first meet a coachee, there is a great deal of information you do not know but, as you get to know each other and build trust, the hidden window becomes smaller and the open window larger, as information is shared.

The fourth 'unknown' quadrant shows things the coachee does not know about themselves and neither does the coach they are working with. In the course of the coaching conversation they may discuss or explore something that reveals new information to both of them. This may trigger personal awareness and growth.

We should thus aim to enlarge the open quadrant and to reduce the others.

## LEARNING EXPERIENTIALLY

Experiential learning refers to learning by doing rather than learning by being told. A well-known way of portraying experiential learning is in the form of a circle. Figure 4 is based on an experiential learning circle given in Kolb (1984).

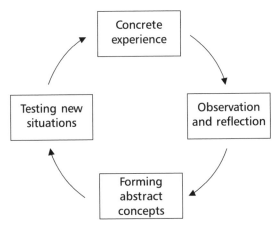

**Fig. 4. An experiential learning circle.**

The coachee first carries out an action and then sees the effect of this action on and in the situation. The coachee then comes to an understanding of these effects in this situation so that, if the same action were taken in similar circumstances, they would be able to anticipate what would follow. These observations and reflections are then brought together into a 'theory' from which new implications for action can be worked out. Finally, this 'theory' is used as a guide to acting in new situations.

Concrete experience validates and tests abstract concepts or 'theories' via feedback from the situation. Although these steps are shown as a circular movement, things may, however, be occurring at the same time. If learning has taken place, then such a process could be seen as a spiral of steps, 'each composed of a circle of planning, action, and fact-finding about the result of the action'.

The following is an example of experiential learning in a coaching situation:

- **Concrete experience**: your coachee has identified that they are having difficulty discussing issues with their boss.
- **Observation and reflection**: your coachee returns to the workplace and observes the interaction between themselves and their boss from both perspectives. They are encouraged to notice what is happening and to reflect on this for the next session.
- **Forming abstract concepts**: your coachee then forms ideas and concepts around the interactions with their boss and brings these to the coaching session.
- **Testing in new or similar situations**: your coachee explores with you how to put these new concepts and/or behaviours into practice, where appropriate.

# 7

# Coaching tools and exercises

This chapter discusses some tools and exercises you could employ in your coaching sessions. Some will be a useful fallback for when you or your coachee become stuck. Others can be used at the start of a session to break the ice.

## THE PREP FORM

One of the best ways for your coachees to plan their sessions is to use the prep form (see Appendix 1). This can be emailed to the coachee before the session and should be returned to you in advance of the session so that you can see what the coachee would like to address or focus on. This will help with the clarity and direction of the session.

## IDENTIFYING YOUR VALUES

As a leader coaching others, it is useful to know your own values and those of your coachees. This will help you to understand what motivates them and will enable you to get to the areas that really make a difference to your relationship.

Figure 5 lists some true values taken from the materials supplied by CoachU and written by Thomas Leonard. Values form the basis of how you approach your life: what you value, and how much you value it, affect your attitudes, beliefs, choices and behaviours.

Do the following exercise for yourself and then ask your coachees to do the same.

## Exercise

*Identifying your values:*

■ *Select ten values that you really live by. Select the words that most appeal to you in your daily life and/or in your job.*

■ *Underline the top four values. A value is a **must** in order for you to be yourself. Part of this step is to be truthful about what you actually value or love to do with your time. This may be the first time you have ever admitted this to yourself. Some of these you will know innately. Others will require some frank 'soul-searching'. Ask yourself: 'Why is this value important enough to me to be a true value?' Write down five specific reasons on a sheet of paper.*

■ *Ask: 'Who am I when I am this value? How do I act? What do I think about? What motivates me?' Write down five specific examples on a piece of paper.*

■ *Ask: 'Who am I not when I am this value? How do I behave? How do I feel about myself? About others? About life?' Write down five specific responses on a piece of paper.*

*When you have your top four values, ask your coach to support you by working towards achieving them.*

## THE WHEEL

Another useful tool is the wheel. This can be adapted to suit almost any situation and can be developed by both the coach and

| Adventure | To create | To lead | Mastery |
|---|---|---|---|
| Risk | Design | Guide | Expert |
| The unknown | Invent | Inspire | Dominate field |
| Thrill | Synthesise | Influence | Adept |
| Danger | Imagination | Cause | Superiority |
| Speculation | Ingenuity | Arouse | Primacy |
| Dare | Originality | Enrol | Pre-eminence |
| Gamble | Conceive | Reign | Greatest |
| Endeavour | Plan | Govern | Best |
| Quest | Build | Rule | Outdo |
| Experiment | Perfect | Persuade | Set standards |
| Exhilaration | Assemble | Encourage | Excellence |
| Venture | Inspire | Model | |

| To catalyse | To contribute | To relate | To win |
|---|---|---|---|
| Impact | Serve | Be connected | Prevail |
| Move forward | Improve | Part of | Accomplish |
| Touch | Augment | community | Attain |
| Turn on | Assist | Family | Score |
| Unstick others | Endow | To unite | Acquire |
| Coach | Strengthen | To nurture | Win over |
| Spark | Facilitate | Be linked | Triumph |
| Encourage | Minister to | Be bonded | Predominate |
| Influence | Grant | Be integrated | Attract |
| Stimulate | Provide | Be with | |
| Energise | Foster | | |
| Alter | Assist | | |

| To discover | To feel | Be sensitive | Be spiritual |
|---|---|---|---|
| Learn | Emote | Tenderness | Be aware |
| Detect | To experience | Touch | Be accepting |
| Perceive | Sense | Perceive | Be awake |
| Locate | To glow | Be present | Relate with God |
| Realise | To feel good | Empathise | Devoting |
| Uncover | Be with | Support | Holy |
| Discern | Energy flow | Show | Honouring |
| Distinguish | In touch with | compassion | Be passionate |
| Observe | Sensations | Respond | Religious |
| | | See | |

| Beauty | Pleasure | To teach | |
|---|---|---|---|
| Grace | Have fun | Educate | |
| Refinement | Be hedonistic | Instruct | |
| Elegance | Sex | Enlighten | |
| Attractiveness | Sensual | Inform | |
| Loveliness | Bliss | Prepare | |
| Radiance | Be amused | Edify | |
| Magnificence | Be entertained | Prime | |
| Gloriousness | Play games | Uplift | |
| Taste | Sports | Explain | |

**Fig. 5. Values.**

coachee. The wheel is a great way to allow your coachees to 'get out of their heads' and to see their thoughts on paper. Many people find having a visual tool helpful and enlightening. Using coloured paper, pens and postcards can also stimulate conversations and can aid the coaching process when people are stuck.

Using the job performance wheel (see Figure 6), ask your coachee to rate themselves from 1 to 10, where the outside of the wheel is a positive 10 and the centre is 0. They should mark their score with a dot on the spoke of the wheel and then join up the dots to get a misshapened circle.

Fig. 6. A job performance wheel.

You should encourage your coachee to focus on any areas they like as most will have an impact on the other areas of the wheel. Support them to see their strengths and to reflect on how to develop areas where they scored poorly. Often coachees will score themselves low but have no evidence to support this low score when questioned by their coach. The leadership wheel (see Figure 7) is used in exactly the same way.

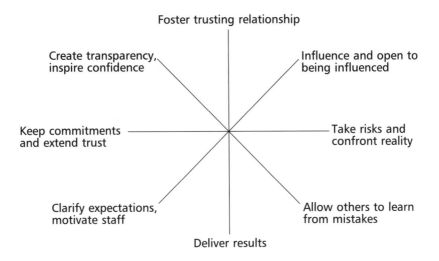

**Fig. 7. A leader's wheel.**

## GETTING TO THE HEART OF LIMITING BELIEFS

As a leader coaching in the workplace, you will sometimes need to confront the limiting beliefs held by your staff. These are beliefs they have held for a number of years and have become old habits. They are often in the form of stories we tell ourselves, such as, 'I am no good at standing up in front of people. Every meeting I go to I always feel anxious and never seem to get my points across succinctly', or 'I don't understand figures and whenever I come to do my accounts I feel a tenseness in my stomach. It generally takes me far longer to do them and then I end up rushing it and making mistakes'.

The key words in the first example are 'no good', 'every', 'always' and 'never'. In the second one they are 'don't understand', 'whenever', 'generally' and 'far longer'. Notice that these words are generalisations. In order to get to the heart of the limiting belief, you should obtain the evidence, to check if the coachee really does have this feeling at 'every' meeting and is 'never' able to get a point across. Of course there will be times when coachees have plenty of evidence to prove their beliefs. After all, this may have given them an excuse or a let-out from having to stand up at meetings or do their accounts. There is usually some kind of payoff!

As their coach, you can encourage your coachee to seek out the positive aspects of the situation. Ideally, try to establish that there have been times when they have made a point successfully at a meeting, or managed to complete their accounts on time.

## Exercise

*By completing this exercise, your coachee may discover new insights. They should ask themselves the following questions:*

- *What evidence do I have to support this belief?*
- *How is this belief less than accurate or exaggerated?*
- *What is keeping this belief helping me to do?*
- *What caused me to cultivate this belief? Where did it come from? So do these assumptions still apply?*
- *Has there ever been a time when this belief did not apply? (In the first example above: 'Have I ever managed to make a useful point at a meeting anywhere?')*

*You should now help your coachee to exchange this belief for an empowering belief.*

*In the example above, for example ('I am able to focus on the time when I was able to make a point at a meeting'):*

- *What past experience can I draw on to support this new belief?*
- *Who do I know who demonstrates this belief?*

- *What will happen if I prevent this new belief from going forward?*
- *What can I do to maintain this belief?*

*At first your coachee may not go along completely with this new belief. The old one may have become a habit, so it is like paddling down a fast-flowing river and then having to change and paddle back up again against the current. As their coach, encourage them to keep trying it out. After they have acquired this new evidence they will be able to build on it and so it will become easier.*

## CONFRONTING THE ENERGY-DRAINERS

Sometimes your coachee may need to confront those things that are currently draining their energy. The following exercise can help them to recognise and plug these energy-drainers.

### Exercise

*Ask your coachees to list ten things that are draining their energy at the moment. Examples may be as follows:*

- *The overflowing in-tray.*
- *The 100 emails.*
- *Endlessly speaking to an employee about their behaviour.*

*For each, ask your coachee to think about three action steps (they don't have to be big ones) that will plug the holes and increase their energy and motivation. If their energy runs out of the cup (see Figure 8), they will need to plug the holes by getting rid of the things that are draining them.*

**Fig. 8. Energy running out of the cup.**

# THE SDOC TOOL

The SDOC tool is like a SWOT analysis but with development areas and challenges! While a SWOT analysis assesses the **S**trengths, **W**eaknesses, **O**pportunities and **T**hreats involved in a project, the SDOC tool assesses someone's **S**trengths, **D**evelopment areas, **O**pportunities and **C**hallenges. This model can be used when coaching individuals and for team coaching.

If you are coaching an individual, ask them to write down their strengths in the area they would like to focus on – and to be bold about this! Then follow this with the development areas they have identified. Next, ask them what they see as their opportunities (or threats) and challenges (see Figure 9).

| Strengths | Development areas |
|---|---|
| | |
| Opportunities | Challenges |
| | |

**Fig. 9. The SDOC tool.**

For teams, the questions are the same but the areas are considered collectively. It may help to ask teams to break into smaller groups and to use large flipchart paper and coloured pens.

## Establishing the goal

Your coachee could now establish their goal for next three months. Ask them to do the following:

- Take a large piece of paper and some coloured pens and draw three large, empty shapes going up the page and almost covering the paper.
- At the top of the page, write your goal in one sentence. Make it an inspiring goal that will really stretch and challenge you. Use descriptive words. 'I'd like to go for promotion' is not very inspiring! Extend this as follows: 'I'd like to take over the role of $x$ so that I could . . . this would enable me to . . .'

## Describing the goal as if it has already been achieved

Now ask your coachee to go forward three months and to write a clear, vivid, detailed description of their goal as if it had already been achieved. They should write this in the top large shape on their paper. They should use bright, inspirational words and detail, and should imagine what they and others will see and hear when they reach their goal.

## What is the current reality of this goal?

Now ask your coachee to write a clear, honest description of the current reality of the goal, without any judgement or analysis. They should write this in the second large shape. This is what they have done so far, if anything.

## Actions arising

Next, they should record the actions and the date by when they will have carried them out in the third large shape on their page.

## Using affirmations

Finally, ask your coachee to write three affirmations related to their goal and desired outcome. Affirmations are very powerful statements that can help coachees to get rid of negative assumptions and beliefs. They are positive, present-tense statements of the desired outcome, written in the first person ('I am, can, have, see, understand, realise, know', etc.). For example:

- I am in my new role and it feels great to be leading the team.
- I now have new challenges and feel the support of the management team.
- I can easily hold this position and am learning all the time.

## INCREASING CONFIDENCE AND SELF-ESTEEM

While the following exercises are not coaching in the purest sense because you are making suggestions, it is often a lack of confidence or self-esteem that may be holding your coachee back. Suggest these exercises but always leave it up to your coachee to decide whether they want to try them or not. Some people enjoy doing them whereas others do not – it's *their* choice.

### Boosting confidence

Even small achievements can boost someone's confidence. Ask your coachee to write a list of all their past achievements and small successes. They should start at their childhood and then slowly come up to the present. Some people find this very difficult. If so, to prompt them, ask the following questions:

- Have you ever helped anyone – even if it was crossing the road or picking something up for them?
- What were your favourite subjects at school? The ones where you won a prize or really shone?
- Have you ever been part of a group where you initiated something that went well?
- What have you made in the past – cooking, woodwork, pottery, art, etc.?
- In your job, what achievements have you realised?

You could ask them to do this at home and then show you their answers at the next session.

### Enhancing self-esteem

Planting the seeds of self-esteem can be very empowering and can greatly enhance your coachee's motivation. Ask them to write down some positive sentences in the *present* tense (affirmations – see above). These may not yet be true but they can be repeated over several weeks to open up possibilities.

For example, someone who is looking for promotion but feels they are not quite up to the challenge might write the following:

- I am reworking my CV so that it shows my true strengths and achievements.
- Some of my key achievements are...
- I am capable of achieving well in...
- People come to me for...
- I currently make a considerable contribution to...
- I am able to carry out $x$ and $y$ with success.
- I have skills in $x$ and $y$ that I can build on.

## VISUALISING

All athletes use visualisation to challenge themselves to greater heights. You could try this with your coachees. For example, one of your coachees wants to make a key presentation to the board of directors but is daunted by the prospect. Ask them to close their eyes and visualise the following:

- Walking into the meeting head held high and feeling confident.
- Standing at the front of the room prepared and rehearsed.
- Delivering the presentation with confidence and a clear voice.
- Handling the questions that may arise with clarity and focus.
- Taking any action points and comments with calmness.
- Walking out of the room feeling the presentation was a success.

Next ask if they would like to act this out, either in the session or at home. The more times they do this, the easier it becomes. As their coach, support them to plan, prepare and practise for the presentation (see my book, *Speaking on Special Occasions*, 2008).

## MAKING DECISIONS

Very often people have tuned out to their own inner wisdom and experience, and so leaders sometimes need to support those people who struggle making decisions. Managers, for example, may find it difficult to trust themselves to come up with the right decision at the right time. As their coach, ask them to think of a small decision: choosing what to wear at a meeting or when to tackle a certain task. Then suggest they close their eyes and 'ask' themselves what they should do. Allow them some moments to explore in a way that may be new to them. When they are ready, ask them the following:

- What was the first thing that came into your mind?
- What did that tell you?
- What would need to happen for you to trust and develop that thought?

This exercise can be done on a regular basis. If your coachees ask themselves the same questions, this will raise their awareness of their inner self and will recreate their ability to make decisions formed from their own knowledge and experience.

## THE TWO POSSIBILITIES

Another very powerful way to decide between two options is to ask your coachee to imagine they have one ball in each hand containing the two options they are trying to chose between. Ask them to weigh the two balls in their hands and to imagine which one is the heavier and less favourable option and which the lighter and, therefore, the option they feel is easier. Ask your coachee to trust the way they are imagining the tasks, and question them as to why one may be heavier than the other. What may this be telling them about the task?

To continue this exercise, explore whether in fact the decision is really only between two options. It may be that these can be combined in some way or that one option can complement the other. The same exercise can then continue as follows:

- Tell your coachee to place the two imaginary balls on the floor at an equal distance from each other (they can draw two balls on two separate pieces of paper if no balls are available).
- Ask them to walk between the two balls (options) and to see if there is a way to combine them. Again, ask them to notice which one is the easier and the one they are drawn to.

In doing this exercise coachees often experience a shift in their thinking, and this can be quite revealing for them. Encourage them to come to a decision by choosing one option or by combining them.

If there are more than two options then this exercise can be done by drawing the options as diagrams on a piece of paper and weighing them to 'feel' which is the heaviest/lightest and so on.

## NEURO-LINGUISTIC PROGRAMMING

Neuro-linguistic programming (NLP) tries to make individuals more aware of how other people may be thinking or feeling. It aims to achieve a high level of empathy between people so that someone can view a situation from another person's perspective.

We all use our senses to experience the world, to create thoughts and to remember events. No sense is used in isolation but we each have a preferred system to represent the world that we use unconsciously. Those systems used for communication are visual, auditory and kinaesthetic. According to NLP, everyone has a set pattern of speaking that reflects their preferred system of representing the world.

A visual person, for example, may say 'Yes, I can see that' or 'Yes, in my view that makes things very clear'. Someone using an auditory system may say 'Yes, that sounds about right' or 'Yes, I hear what you are saying'. Someone using the kinaesthetic system may say 'Yes, I have a better grasp on that now' or 'Um, that feels about right'.

Someone who is very visual may uses such phrases as 'I'm not seeing a way through here'. You could reply by asking them the following:

- What would enable you to clarify this?
- What's blocking your view here?

Such people would also respond well to visual tools and methods, such as a SDOC diagram or a goal sheet (see above).

Someone who is auditory may say: 'He always sounds so angry when he approaches me.' A coaching reflection may be: 'So you find it hard to listen to his anger?' A question may be: 'What do you tell yourself when he's angry?'

If your coachee uses a kinaesthetic system, they may say: 'It just doesn't feel right. I'm uncomfortable in those situations.' You could reflect back with: 'You obviously feel a certain amount of discomfort in this situation. What would make you feel more supported?'

It will not always be possible to use your coachee's ideal system and, indeed, it is often the case that people employ a variety of systems to match a particular situation. However, just having an awareness of their preferred system can give your sessions a greater depth of understanding.

## Perceptual positions

Perceptual positions is an NLP technique that requires some practice. It can often create a new awareness, even when someone wants to hold on to their own view of the world.

### Exercise

*Think for a moment of a personal experience where your interaction with someone broke down or your coachee told you of a situation where the communication didn't go as well as they would have liked. Your coachee may have said something like the following:*

- *I can never seem to say the right thing.*
- *I was not intending to . . .*
- *They always seem to get offended.*
- *Their reaction is always unpredictable.*

*What they generally mean is that they would like the 'other person' to change or alter the way they behave. In such cases you should try to enable your coachee to understand that the problem may lie in their own behaviour.*

*Depending on how directive you are in your approach and how challenging your coachee has asked you to be, you could begin with the following:*

- *How do you think the other person felt when you said...?*
- *What other phrase could you use that may work more effectively?*
- *What impact do you think your action had in this situation?*
- *If you had been on the receiving end of this statement/suggestion/ question, what reaction would you have had?*

*If you feel your coachee is beginning to see that their behaviour may be the cause of the problem, ask, 'Would you like to try a method that may help you to see things differently?' It is essential to obtain their permission because this process can be very illuminating.*

*If your coachee is willing, you can begin to explain the perceptual positions:*

- *self*
- *other*
- *non-judgemental observer.*

*Ask them to imagine the problem. If they are willing, ask them to close their eyes and really to 'see' the situation unfolding again. Then say, 'Think carefully about what you said and the other person's reaction. Really hear what you said and what they said. How did it feel?' (If your coachee is prepared so to do and would find it helpful, they can say their own words out loud as they said them at the time.) This is the 'self' part of exercise.*

*Now move on to the 'other' part. Ask your coachee,*

*'Now visualise yourself being in that person's body. Take on their stance and really be as they are. You may like to sit in another chair to take on their character and demeanour. As that other person, look back at yourself as you were then. See the interaction and imagine the conversation from*

*the other person's point of view. Pay attention to what you see and hear and how it feels.'*

*(If your coachee is willing, you can ask them to say the other person's words as they said them at the time.)*

*Move on to the 'observer' part. Ask your coachee to imagine the conversation again and say,*

*'This time you are a neutral observer. View the conversation from above and watch the interaction between those two people as they were then. Really hear the words and feel the emotion between them. Ask yourself if there is anything you can learn from that.'*

*Finish by asking your coachee any or all of the following:*

- *Did you notice anything as the non-judgemental observer that could help this communication next time?*
- *What did you notice that may have contributed to the outcome of this conversation?*
- *Is there anything you could do differently next time to turn this situation around?*

*You may like to try repeating the perceptual positions again employing the amended behaviour. This helps to embed the learning for your coachee. However, this may not be necessary as many people are surprised at the way this process sheds light on the situation.*

## EMPLOYING PSYCHOMETRIC TOOLS

Psychometric tests and questionnaires are designed to measure an individual's abilities, knowledge, personality, aptitude, etc., and they have long been used, for example, in the recruitment and selection of staff. They can also be of value when you are coaching people who are facing promotion or a career change. I employ a variety of personality questionnaires to enable my coachees to:

■ discover their underlying needs and core values;
■ uncover their strengths and career goals;
■ clarify their preferred ways of working;
■ identify their leadership styles and preferences; and
■ understand rejection or accept failure at an interview.

These tools are particularly helpful when you want to establish your coachee's preferred learning style or working environment. People are often more tolerant of their staff or adopt a different style with their boss when they have clarified their own styles of learning and working and those of their co-workers. They see situations in a different light, and this enhances the quality of their relationships and communication. If these tools are used to reflect on a failed application for promotion, the feedback your coachee receives from this exercise can be very valuable the next time round. This feedback should be sensitive and constructive and should encourage your coachee to learn from the experience.

These tools should not be employed to put people in boxes and, because there is a variety of tests and questionnaires, you should find out which suit you and your coachees the best.

## USING CLEAN LANGUAGE

'Clean language' was devised by the psychotherapist, David Grove. He wanted a way to keep his assumptions, as far as possible, out of his interactions with his clients so that he could work directly with their perceptions. Grove watched other practitioners at work and analysed transcripts of them working with their clients. He realised that these practitioners were subtly rewording what their clients were saying and felt that this was robbing the clients of some of their experience. He decided, therefore, to keep his clients' words intact by repeating them verbatim, and he also considered what questions he could ask his clients that would contain fewer presuppositions, while still directing attention to aspects of their experience that seemed to merit exploration.

'What are you thinking?', for example, presupposes that a person is thinking something and limits their possible responses. So Grove 'cleaned' the question to become: 'Are you thinking anything?' Later, he dropped the word 'thinking' (and the word 'feeling') and used an even cleaner question: 'Is there anything else about $x$?'

A statement such as 'I want you to tell me how you feel about $x$' shifts a person's attention back and forth (I – you – me – you – $x$), so Grove removed all pronouns, unless they were part of what the person was talking about. 'Tell me more' also turned into 'Is there anything else?' He also wanted to be specific about where he was directing a person's attention, so he introduced the word 'that' into many of his questions: 'What kind of $x$ is that $x$?' Since a person's experience is happening now (even if they're recalling a memory), he framed all his questions in the present tense. Finally, he wanted people to stay in their experience, so he joined his questions into what they were saying by prefacing them with the word 'and' (see the examples below).

'Symbolic modelling' is the name given by Penny Tompkins and James Lawley to the model they devised after working with Grove over several years to discover what he was doing to achieve such good results. They combined his ideas with those from other fields (such as cognitive linguistics, systems thinking and NLP), to produce a model that could be taught to others to enable them to achieve the same kinds of results as Grove had done.

You start the process by asking one of the following questions to identify a particular perception (where $x$ = the person's word or words):

■ And what would you like to have happen?
■ And what's that like?
■ And how do you know $x$?
■ And then what happens?
■ And what happens/happened just before $x$?
■ And is there a relationship between $x$ and $y$?
■ And what needs to happen for $x$ to happen?

If at all possible, start by asking: 'What would you like to have happen?' to identify what your coachee wants and to clarify this perception first. You can then employ this information to help you decide what it might be useful for your coachee to pay attention to.

Next, you keep your coachee's attention on what they have said by asking two or three developing questions:

■ And is there anything else (about $x$)?
■ And what kind of $x$ is that $x$?
■ And where is $x$?

Finally, you repeat the above two steps.

Although there are only a few developing questions to choose from, when you combine them with your coachee's own words every question is unique. Asking these questions helps to slow a person down and gets them to think about what they really mean by the words they've used, particularly the metaphors they employ to express their perception of the world. Clean language is not about making someone change, however. You are simply helping them to explore and clarify their thinking. If change happens, it is a by-product of them having this additional information.

Marian Way, a clean language coach and trainer, has kindly contributed this list of the benefits of clean language coaching:

- It makes people think things through for themselves. They own the ideas they come up with and are much more likely to take action than if they rely on you for suggestions.
- The ideas people generate through the use of metaphor are generally quite inventive and idiosyncratic. They are a real 'fit' with the person who generates them.
- Coachees get a lot more than good ideas from clean language coaching. They learn to understand the structure of their own thinking and behaviour patterns. Over time, they learn how to pay attention to their own patterns as they happen, and can work out ways to change unwanted ones.
- There is no resistance from the coachee. Since you are only using their words combined with the clean language questions, there is nothing to resist. People find their own metaphors infinitely fascinating.

(See Appendix 3 for a case study on clean language.)

## EMPLOYING ALTERNATIVE METHODS TO COACHING

While coaching and mentoring are excellent ways of encouraging people to grow and learn, they are by no means the only methods and, often, a combination of coaching and mentoring and other methods is needed. Some of these other methods are:

- training;
- consultancy;
- shadowing;
- team days;
- role plays;
- appraisals;
- performance management;
- personal development plans; and
- monitoring and feedback.

## Training

Training aims to give people information and additional skills, and it involves input, practice and feedback. Training usually takes one or two days or a weekend, although some qualification courses can last for several months. One of the drawbacks of training is that what is learnt is often implemented for a week or so, but then forgotten as people revert to what is more familiar to them. New skills and knowledge take time to embed, and this is where coaching and mentoring really can help to consolidate training.

## Consultancy

A consultant offers advice as an expert in a particular field. They use in-depth questioning to gain a full understanding of the way an organisation works. They then collate this information and employ it to suggest a recommended course of action.

## Shadowing

Shadowing is a useful way to support people who are new to their role or who need to learn a new skill. It enables them to observe, ask questions and learn without the pressure of actually doing the job. Combined with mentoring, shadowing can be very effective, and coaching can also be undertaken after the person has been in role for a few weeks to ensure the learning has been embedded.

## Team days

It is often not possible for teams to find out about their colleagues' real values, attitudes and experiences because work pressures offer little time for more than a brief interaction. A team day can be a real boost to a team's morale and motivation, and a coaching-style of team day is particularly effective. The coach can act as a catalyst for the team to come up with ideas and plans. If you give your team a non-judgemental, positive space in which to explore their ideas, you will encourage their thoughts to flow.

As in a one-to-one coaching session, you should ask questions, reflect and listen deeply to their suggestions and expertise. If the day is held away from work in a relaxed environment, this will achieve the best results.

## Role play

Role play is an effective way of practising for a new job, for confronting a difficult member of staff, for learning a new technique and for seeing things from a different perspective. The chief drawbacks of role play are that many people are uncomfortable 'playing a role' and that it cannot predict all the possibilities in a real-life situation.

## Appraisals

A appraisal should be a rewarding conversation between you as a manager/coach and a member of your staff. If you apply a coaching style to appraisals, you should really get to know your staff's needs and concerns, although some appraisals may simply be to give feedback on your staff's performance, to advise them on company policies or to update them on new products or services.

Share the information in a relaxed conversation: be curious, listen as well as inform and, as far as possible, give feedback by enabling your employee to state their side of the story. If you are confronting someone about their behaviour, make sure you have the evidence and stick to the facts.

## Performance management

What are your measures for good performance? What standards have you set as benchmarks for people's own self-assessment? Everyone performs better when they feel valued and supported. Are your organisational goals/values visible and do they align to your own personal goals/values and those of your team? Are your employees encouraged to collect their own evidence and to think about their own achievements before a performance management review?

Performance management is usually carried out within a framework of:

- planning;
- setting objectives;
- monitoring progress;

- giving feedback;
- reviewing; and
- forward planning.

A coaching style can be used throughout the process to enable your staff to take ownership of, and responsibility for, their performance.

## Personal development plans

Personal development plans are ideal for coaching. Most companies encourage their staff to consider and continuously to update their personal development plans and, if you use a coaching style, this can greatly facilitate the process. You can help your staff to take ownership of their ideas and their own continuing professional development.

## Monitoring and feedback

Monitoring need not be intrusive. You may, for example, decide to set up a brief interview to find out how things are going, or simply have an email exchange to check on progress. As a manager, you should be aware of agreed actions and of any areas that require your input. Giving your staff the opportunity to feed back to you at specific times will place the responsibility so to do firmly on them.

When giving feedback, it is essential to support this with evidence and to use non-judgemental language, such as, 'I noticed that...', 'I realised that...' and 'It seems to me that...' Naturally you should be truthful, and this involves being open and frank with people when necessary.

The way in which feedback is handled is vital to your staff's growth. People lose motivation if they are undervalued, so any small achievement needs to be recognised and commented on. When bringing up development areas, avoid delivering them as a personal criticism but, instead, use clear constructive guidelines on how and what could be improved. You should back up your comments with facts and, possibly, with evidence from 360° feedback or from observations from other colleagues.

Some of the key skills of giving effective feedback are as follows (see also Chapter 8):

- Checking the consequences of a person's thoughts/feelings/ actions.
- Exploring a person's own understanding of their thoughts/ feelings/actions.
- Reflecting the person's own feelings and thoughts.
- Noticing and reflecting behaviours.
- Summarising the person's views and feelings.
- Expressing constructive ways of development and improvement.

# 8

# Effective communication skills

## CREATING A GOOD COACHING RELATIONSHIP

In order to make a coachee or mentee feel comfortable in the sessions, it is necessary to create a rapport between you, to build up a relationship of trust and safety. It is all very well to set goals and to discuss targets but, without a strong relationship, the sessions will not have the desired outcomes. Creating the space where people feel nurtured and really heard is a vital part of your role. When *mentoring* managers be aware that they are generally looking for further expertise, advice and guidance. When *coaching* managers, bear in mind that what they are looking for is a true partner: someone with whom they can share concerns and admit failings without judgement.

As a manager/coach, spend some time before the coaching sessions to centre yourself and to rid yourself of any negative thoughts or preconceptions. This will allow you to put aside any pre-knowledge of your coachee you may have and will enable the session to be totally non-judgemental. This is easier said than done, but with practice, it can be achieved.

As a coach, tap into your authentic self and be genuinely present in the moment for your coachees. This way you will release their potential and allow them to face their challenges with a true partner. In a coaching role you will be standing back from the role of the 'expert'. You will need to believe that the person you are supporting will come up with their own answers and solutions. This can be challenging as you may have built up an unfavourable picture of your coachee and may find it difficult to believe in their potential. Everyone, however, has the potential to grow and develop in their own way. This may not be the way you expected, though, and so you may have to block out your own internal chatter, such as 'That will never work' or 'Oh dear, that's really not the way I would do it'.

## Case study

*Jane was the principal of a language school in Cheltenham and she had asked me to coach her as she was feeling overloaded. The following is an extract from our first session:*

**Coach**: *What would you like to use this session for today?*

**Jane**: *I feel totally overstretched and my workload has increased as the school has expanded. I am feeling very tired and can't seem to keep on top of everything.*

**Coach**: *So you have an additional workload that is making you feel tired. Tell me a little more about what it is you can't keep on top of* (using her own words).

**Jane**: *Well, this week, I need to speak to a couple of my agents. I need to organise the teaching schedule, prepare for our up-and-coming inspection and recruit a couple of new teachers. Preparing for the inspection is taking so much of my time* (sighs).

**Coach**: *It sounds like the impending inspection is causing you to feel pressured. What needs to happen so that you can feel more on top of* *things?* (No advice, just reflecting and putting a very open question.)

*Jane: Well, it would be nice to get someone to take over some of the process but no one has the experience really.* (Believes that she is the only person who can do these tasks effectively.)

**Coach***: So you have no one who can take on that responsibility?* (Challenges that assumption by reflecting her thoughts.)

*Jane: No . . .* (thinks for a few moments) *My director of studies, Kate, is very capable but I can't see her being able to understand all that is required. She works so differently to me.*

**Coach***: Yes, I can see that you think it would be a lot for Kate. In what way does she work differently?* (Encouraging her to think about the way Kate works.)

*Jane: Well, she's very organised and good at sorting things out . . . umm. She's good at systems but less effective when it comes to dealing with staff. I suppose I could get her to take on some of the organisational tasks.*

**Coach***: What specific tasks do you think she could take on?* (Helping her to think clearly about where Kate can help.)

*Jane: I could ask her what she felt she was able to organise in terms of the inspection. There are guidelines that she can follow and I could talk her though those. There are a number of processes that she could put in place for the teaching staff. Yes, perhaps she would do things differently but actually her skills are quite well suited to setting up systems and processes.*

*During the coaching session, Jane was encouraged to think about how she could best use the skills and talents of her Director of Studies. Often, as managers or leaders of organisations, you believe your way is best and, of course, that can sometimes be true. However, unless you are prepared to take a few risks and delegate, you will become overloaded and your staff will not learn and grow. In her discussion with Kate the following day, Jane realised that she could give Kate a great deal more responsibility than she had expected. Kate had a much better understanding than Jane had realised, and this not only freed Jane up but also motivated Kate to take on more responsibility for the inspection. Sometimes just showing your coachee that you believe in their potential can encourage them to be both creative and more effective.*

## USING APPROPRIATE LANGUAGE

The language of coaching is, at its best, simple and straightforward. Short, curious questions such as the following are some of the most effective:

- What else?
- Is there anything else about that?
- What do you mean exactly?
- What needs to happen now?
- How do you feel about that?

When reflecting to the coachee what they have said, it is very effective to use their language, as this helps them to understand their own meaning.

## Case study

*John was being coached and was explaining that he felt a* lack of confidence *in a particular situation. His coach reflected, 'I heard from your comments just now that you feel you lack self-esteem.'*

*To which John replied, 'Oh no, I am just not confident in this situation. It has nothing to do with self-esteem!'*

*A more suitable reflection by the coach using John's language would have been, 'So you feel that, in this kind of situation, you lack confidence'.*

*When the coach reflected in this way, John could hear what he himself had said and could then decide if this was true or needed further exploration from the coach. For example,*

- *What do you mean by confidence in this situation?*
- *What would you be doing if you were more confident?*
- *How would that make you feel?*

Obviously when reflecting it is useful to be aware of the coachee's language, but you should avoid sounding patronising or parrot-like! The sensitive use of appropriate language is what you are after here (see also the section on clean language in Chapter 7).

It is unhelpful to employ jargon and technical language that are unfamiliar to your coachee. In the workplace, it is unwise to assume that others will know the terminology of your own department or job role. It can, however, help to know the kind of language your coachee prefers to use (see the section on neuro-linguistic programming in Chapter 7).

## LISTENING AT A DEEP LEVEL

When coaching or mentoring, consider the three levels of listening:

- superficial
- active
- deep.

**Superficial listening** is when you hear what is being said but have other thoughts and questions in your mind. You may be speaking to a colleague while listening to a more interesting telephone conversation across the room, for example. Or you may be running through the main points of a presentation in your mind while a colleague is telling you about a topic you are not really interested in. You are listening with only one ear and the details pass you by.

**Active listening** is when you are engaged in the conversation and may give visual clues to the speaker that you are paying attention. You may nod in agreement or raise your eye-brows. You may use phrases such as, 'Yes, I see' or 'Umm, that sounds like a good idea'. You are listening with both ears but your mind may be wanting to ask a question or to explain your particular point of view. You would like to jump in with a suggestion or let them know you had a similar experience.

**Deep listening** is when you are totally engaged with the person who is speaking. Your focus is entirely on them and their words, thoughts and feelings. You are conscious of their body language and speaking patterns. There are no thoughts or suggestions in your mind as you are being totally non-judgemental and allowing them to use the space to speak and explore their situation.

To have someone listen to you in this way is very empowering. At first, people may feel uncomfortable as it can seem a little unusual. However, if you explain that this is the best way for them to find their own solutions, they will quickly become accustomed to it.

Many coachees feel that this is the best part of coaching. For the first time they are really being 'heard' and their ideas and thoughts are valued and listened to at a very deep level.

In coaching terms, your own state of mind is called your 'presence'. The way you turn up for your coachees will determine the outcome of the session and how well your coachees feel listened to. If you are 'still' in mind and body you will enable your coachees to expand their thinking, and you will notice more of what *is not* said during the session. This may often be the real insight.

## ASKING EFFECTIVE QUESTIONS

One of the key skills in coaching and mentoring is to ask effective questions. If you are new to coaching, you do not need to have a list of questions in front of you. Nor do you need to feel that your questions are the 'right' ones. There are no 'right' or 'wrong' questions, just questions *that arise from your coachee and their world*. All you need to do is listen at a deep level and the questions will flow naturally. When you are acting as a coach, you are concentrating on your coachee's language and style. You are listening at a level that enables you to ask the right question *for them*.

### Using open questions

Some of the most powerful open questions begin with 'What' – such questions allow the individual to expand on their thinking. For example:

- *What* else can you say about that?
- *What* kind of $x$ is that? (Use their word.)
- *What* would that involve?

- Anything else?
- *What* needs to happen now?
- *What* else?

If your coachee says, '*I feel that my time management needs improvement*', you could ask, 'What aspect of *time management* exactly do you *feel needs improvement*?' Later in the session you could use other use simple questions, such as:

- *What* needs to happen now?
- *Who* else may be involved?
- *How* could you take this forward?

You will notice that, with all these *what, who, how*, etc., questions, there is an assumption that the coachee will know the answers. It is important for the person being coached to have the space and time to consider, without any suggestions from the coach. When you are supporting an individual to take ownership of their answers and possible actions, this freedom to think is vital. There may be silences where you feel the need to jump in with a second question or a prompt, but avoid doing so! This may be the first time your coachee has had the opportunity to really consider the issue. *Give them time to think things through.* Resist the urge to fill the gap with your knowledge or advice, and be prepared to be surprised when your coachee comes up with an answer. It may not be *your* answer, but it is usually the right one *for them*.

Where possible, give them the benefit of the doubt – their way may just be better or more effective than yours. Allowing them to discover the right way by learning from their mistakes will increase their self-knowledge and awareness. Naturally, there may be occasions when you will need to head them away from certain situations. This can also be done by feeding back to them what they propose, and by adding challenging and incisive questions while keeping your voice neutral:

- *What* exactly do you think this (*x* – use their words) would achieve?
- *How* would you go about this (*x* – use their words) precisely?
- *What* results would you expect?
- *What* impact might this have?
- *What* other possibilities could you consider?

At all times you will need to be aware of your tone of voice and stress patterns. Ideally, your tone should be neutral, and you should not indicate your feelings by emphasising certain words to make your coachee feel pressured. This may take more time initially but, if you allow people to expand their thinking in this way, you will be supporting them to grow. They will develop their skills and not feel the need to come to you for advice at all times of the day. This is particularly important when you are leading an organisation and need time to focus on your own role.

If you really feel that the solutions they have come up with will definitely fail (do you really know that?), or if you feel what they propose will definitely have a negative impact, one way forward is to say, '*I have some advice I think would be useful here. Shall we discuss all the options on the table?*' It is just possible they have an idea you may not have considered, or they may have a different take on things. By involving the individual in the discussion and really allowing their views to be considered, they will feel they had a useful part to play and will go away motivated.

## Limiting beliefs/assumptions

When you are involved in a one-to-one coaching session with a member of staff, it is useful to ask questions that will address limiting beliefs and assumptions (see Chapter 7).

Getting to the heart of the issues and blocks will help to unlock your coachee's potential. Powerful questions using your coachee's language can really get to the crux of what is holding them back.

### Case study

*In this case study, a line manager (LM) is coaching an employee (E) new to their role. The employee has been reluctant to start on her annual appraisals and has asked for a coaching session.*

**LM**: *You mentioned you would like to focus this session on your annual appraisals that are coming up?*

**E**: *Yes, er . . . I do.*

**LM**: *What would you like to discuss in this session?*

**E**: *Well, I'm not really sure.*

**LM**: *You sound uncertain. What are you not sure about?* (Using coachee's language.)

**E**: *I'm not very good at appraisals.*

**LM**: *What part of the process are you not good at?*

**E**: *I don't feel very confident about any of it, to be honest.*

**LM**: *What would make you more confident?* (Using their word.)

**E**: *Well, I suppose some kind of training in appraisals would help.*

*LM: So you feel you need further training? Anything else I can support you with?*

*E: Yes, to be frank I have never done appraisals before.* (Sensing that the line manager is being non-judgemental and supportive, she comes out with the real problem.)

*LM: I see. No wonder you were uncertain* (no judgement). *Where shall we go from here?* (Gives her back the responsibility for her actions.)

*E: Well, I have seen that there is appraisal training I could enrol on. Could you set me up with a mentor who could give me some guidance over the next couple of weeks?*

*LM: Yes, of course. When will you have completed your training?* (Obtains commitment.)

*By allowing the employee time to reflect, this line manager was able to get to the heart of the problem.*

## GIVING EFFECTIVE FEEDBACK

Effective feedback is a very empowering technique. If given without thought, however, it can also be very damaging. As a manager or leader, you will have had plenty of practice in giving feedback. In a coaching session, feedback should be sensitive, appropriate, factual and specific. For example:

*Manager/coach*: Sam, I noticed that you were great at the last meeting, your comments were well received.

This is an unhelpful piece of feedback because it reveals nothing about the coachee's skills or knowledge. It is vague, and the coachee has nothing to build on.

*Manager/coach*: Sam, you really spoke with authority and gave a convincing argument at the meeting. The comments you made on the safety issues were very relevant. In my view that's a significant improvement.

How much more empowering the second feedback would have been. The coachee would have taken away the facts that:

- they can speak with authority;
- they can be convincing and relevant;
- they showed their knowledge;
- their coach feels they have improved.

The comments made in the second feedback were helpful and relevant. The coach's observations also served to empower the coachee further.

Some techniques for giving effective feedback include the following:

- Repeating key words and phrases used by your coachee (with sensitivity).
- Reflecting your coachee's feelings, thus allowing them to feel understood (empathy not sympathy).
- Reflecting your coachee's thinking to help them to clarify their thoughts.
- Reflecting your coachee's behaviour to check if they think this is appropriate and, if so, to support and encourage them.

- Reflecting what your coachee is doing so they can see if this is useful/necessary.
- Paraphrasing your coachee's current thoughts, feelings and behaviour to support progress.
- Summarising your coachee's views so they can see things objectively.
- Summarising your coachee's feelings and/or actions to gain clarity.
- Checking the consequences of your coachee's thoughts/feelings/actions.
- Checking your coachee's own understanding of their thoughts/feelings/actions.
- Being open and honest about what you (as a coach) feel is happening in the relationship.

Areas to avoid when giving feedback include the following:

- Ignoring key words and phrases and substituting your own words.
- Telling your coachee what/how they *should* feel or think.
- Telling your coachee what they should do, as this may not be appropriate for them in their situation.
- Telling your coachee how to behave – and/or not acknowledging their behaviour.
- Subtly emphasising your priorities rather than focusing on your coachee's priorities.
- Creating an imbalance between the company's goals and those of your coachee.
- Replacing their views with your views.
- Not expressing and not being honest about how you feel about your coachee/their situation/your understanding of your coachee.

■ Not checking your coachee's understanding of the consequences of their actions.

■ Not checking your coachee's understanding of their thoughts/actions/feelings.

■ Not using your integrity; abusing your power as a coach.

## COMMUNICATING NON-VERBALLY

Asking effective and appropriate questions, reflecting your coachee's words and ideas, summarising and clarifying are all part of professional communication, but what about the non-verbal clues that coaches should be aware of to inform their practice? We all have a body language that is unique to each of us, and there are vital clues to a coachee's feelings in their body language you will observe during coaching sessions. For example:

■ A movement of their body while sitting in a chair.

■ A head bent forward, with eyes down.

■ Eyes up and to the right/left.

■ A deep sigh or cough.

While you should not read too much into body language (someone may just be uncomfortable or be thinking), it is useful to develop an awareness of the way people react and to trust your gut feelings. Often a coachee will be smiling, apparently quite happy with a question. However, you can pick up discomfort or unease in a quick change of position in their chair or a downward glance. Deep sighs can be a sign that people are struggling with a problem, or feeling fed up or tired.

It can be very liberating to your coachee when you pay attention to a deep sigh before a remark or response. For example:

Coach:      So that's your final decision, Mike?

Coachee:    Yes. (*Sighs*) I suppose so.

Coach:      Oh, tell me more about. (*Sighs as the coachee did.*)

Coachee:    Umm yes, it all feels a bit heavy and difficult. (*He looks down and to his left.*)

Coach:      (*Looks down and to the left.*) What's heavy and difficult down there?

In this way the coach enters the coachee's worldview and helps them to understand what they are feeling and experiencing. This needs practice and sensitivity, so new coaches be wary!

You can find out more about recognising body language by taking a course in neuro-linguistic programming (NLP) (see Chapter 7). Pacing and mirroring are useful NLP coaching techniques when applied sensitively and unobtrusively.

## Pacing and mirroring

Pacing and mirroring can produce amazing results when you are handling strong emotions. There will be times when the people you are coaching or mentoring turn up for a session exhibiting strong feelings or emotions. It is completely useless to start any kind of professional conversation when people need to get something off their chest. During a coaching session, it is helpful to give people the opportunity to unwind and air their concerns. Such freedom can unleash some surprising emotions. This is where pacing and mirroring can really help you to stay with someone and eventually to calm them down so that the session can start.

If your coachee is angry, there is no sense in saying, 'Calm down' or 'Please keep your voice down'. This will only make matters worse. If you are sitting and your coachee enters and starts walking up and down obviously distressed, stand up so that you are level with them, and use their language and almost match their tone of voice. For example:

*Coach (head teacher of a school)*: Morning Michele

*Coachee (a member of her leadership team)*: Morning... I cannot for the life of me understand why this delivery hasn't arrived. We have the sports day on Tuesday and all the prizes and awards were in that order. It's just not good enough. (*Paces up and down.*) I am at a loss as to what to do.

*Coach (standing now and using the same tone and pace of speech)*: Yes, the sports day is almost upon us and all the prizes and awards should have arrived, as you say. (*This lets the coachee know her coach understands. Then, with the pace slightly slower and with emphasis on the word 'could'*) Is there something you could do?

*Coachee (still angry but a little less so)*: Yes, calling them with the threat of no orders in future might get things moving! Still, we need them here now. People need to get everything organised.

*Coach (slightly slower and calmer)*: Yes, that's crucial. What needs to happen so everything can be organised in time? (*Coach sits down. This seems natural and appropriate.*)

*Coachee*: Well (*sighs deeply, looks calmer*), I could get Julie to phone them and give them a deadline. She could also contact the other supplier we use to see how quickly they can get the order to us. The staff will just have to get in early on Monday to get things organised.

*Coach*: Anything else?

*Coachee*: Yes (*she sits down*) I could do with a coffee – any available?

By acknowledging the frustration and accepting the coachee's emotion, the coach was able to mirror her stance, reflect her tone of voice and slowly enable the coachee to become calmer. This takes patience and sensitivity as to overdo vocal pacing and mirroring can seem patronising. If you create the right balance and stay focused on your coachee and their language, this can, however, be a powerful engagement. When I first came across this technique I was very wary of it, but it really can have a significant result when done with no judgement and a genuine willingness to support your coachee.

## Being aware of your own body language

As a coach it is useful to be aware of the signals you are giving out. If you arrive at a coaching session rushed or feeling unprepared, your coachee will soon pick this up and the session will not be as productive. Notice your own body language and adjust it accordingly. Do you move about in your chair or are you still and calm during the sessions? Do you lean forward when you are coaching or do you sit back relaxed? By paying attention to your own non-verbal signals, you will become more effective and the sessions will flow.

People often align themselves automatically when in conversation with a colleague or someone they trust. On the coach training courses we run, I have regularly observed that, after a few moments, people are sitting in a similar position during the practice sessions. This helps both parties to feel more at ease.

## PRESENCE AND SILENCE

Allowing your coachee to reflect, think through or just to take time to answer is one of the most valuable parts of a coaching session. Many coachees have expressed the immense relief they felt when they were given the space and time to think.

We are constantly surrounded by noise. Indeed, in today's world it is increasingly difficult to find a space where there is total silence. In this environment it is little wonder that people experience a feeling of relief when they are given the opportunity to have a thinking space. For this reason it is important for a coach to allow that space to grow and expand. This may mean you are both sitting in silence for several minutes without speaking. You should be prepared for your coachee to use this time to extend their creative thinking outside the usual constraints. This trust in the process is a vital element of a successful outcome for your coachee.

Consider for a moment the occasions when you had real quality time to think over a problem or issue. The term 'Sleep on it' is no empty phrase. When you sleep you are calm and relaxed. Your mind has the space and peace to come up with solutions and ideas that, in the waking world, are not possible. If, as a coach, you can create a quiet space for your coachee to think, you will enable them to be more creative. Whether or not you are coaching your staff, or you are a more junior manager coaching your boss, all individuals will welcome this precious time.

A senior manager of an IT company where coaching has been established had the following to report:

*❝After the first five coaching sessions I had been given the time to think about where I was taking the company. The ideas I came up with were surprising and I was excited by the possibilities that came to me. Shortly after the fifth session I went on holiday with my wife to the Swiss Alps. It was amazingly peaceful, high up in the mountains and I found myself thinking more deeply about some of my ideas. On my return my coach suggested I use this peaceful place to 'go to' in my mind when I needed to think over key issues or ideas. Having the silence in the sessions and the peaceful place I can tap into whenever I like has helped me significantly. It has eased my stress and enabled me to think more clearly about my business ideas.* ❞

Silence is the silver thread that enables clear thoughts to emerge and reconnect from hidden sources. It is the peaceful place that can be a catalyst for the best ideas and the most profound revelations.

The sessions will not be as productive if you bring your own baggage into them. Make time to centre yourself by taking deep breaths and relaxing before your coaching sessions. Allow your own knowledge of your coachee and any preconceived ideas to drift from your mind. This way you will be able to listen and truly focus on what your coachee brings to the session. If you are a manager who is using coaching skills but who has not been trained as a coach, try the following exercise.

## Exercise

*Before a coaching session, give yourself* at least *10 minutes to prepare. During this time, allow any irritations or negative thoughts to drift away. Think of a place where you always feel peaceful. Allow your tensions to be released, breath deeply and focus on the individual you are about to coach and* their *needs:*

■ *Remove judgements or assumptions you may be making about the individual.*

■ *Believe that your coachee has the answers to their own issues and can grow and learn.*

■ *Think about the potential this individual has and how you can create a positive experience for them.*

Only when you are in the right frame of mind can you be a truly effective coach. The energy you create in your own space will be transmitted to others. Doing this exercise and using the silence will enhance your coachee's motivation and will allow them to be creative. The energy you create for your coachee will enable them to give their best and to come up with solutions and ideas that will have lasting results.

If as a coach you are able to allow people time and creative space they will often amaze both themselves and you as coach.

# 9

# Analysing communication to identify meaning

As a coach, it is helpful to be aware of your own prejudices, and you should know what kind of behaviours and preconceptions in social and business settings you consider the norm. Once you are clear about this, you can relate it to how others see the world. You are also advised to consider why others may see things differently from you, and knowing the facts that have shaped those attitudes and/or behaviours will greatly inform your coaching. This is one of the reasons why coaches talk about the value of being non-judgemental.

## AVOIDING MISUNDERSTANDINGS

In many countries, frank and open discussion is encouraged. People say what is in their minds and don't hold back. They believe that to hide your feelings is to be dishonest and sly. If you had grown up in such a society you might be naturally suspicious of someone who kept their feelings to themselves or was holding back in a coaching session. You might find that their lack of open responses caused a reaction in you so that your tone of voice changed or you became irritated. By being aware of your own feelings and attitudes, you can keep reactions such as this to a minimum.

I remember clearly when I lived in Switzerland that I found it very difficult to accept the way people communicated. They would greet me in a friendly way in the street but then would seldom invite me into their homes unless I had an appointment. I took it as a personal affront until I realised that this is part of their culture. They like to prepare, make things special and organise everything in advance for their guests. Once I began to visit, having made a previous arrangement, I was made to feel welcome and I was well looked after.

When I worked in Asia I learnt that people often hide their true feeling to 'save face' and that, for example, 'Yes, I see' could often mean that someone did not really understand at all. This meant taking a completely different approach in order to build trust and rapport. As soon as people felt completely 'safe', they learnt to be open with me and the relationship between us flourished.

Everyone can misunderstand people, especially if they are talking in general or being non-specific. This is where stepping in for clarification can be helpful both for the coach and coachee. Sometimes you may feel the urge to give advice or suggestions to people, but when in a coaching role, you should check and contain this tendency whenever possible. The only exception to this is when you may want to share part of your coaching toolkit or a coaching model with your coachee to enhance their understanding of the process.

## UNCOVERING THE TRUTH

Your strengths as a coach are to be able to listen, paraphrase and reframe. This should be balanced by healthy interpersonal boundaries which mean that any questions you put are relevant to the task at hand and are not unnecessarily intrusive or inappropriate. For example:

*Coach*: You asked for this session to reflect on your team leadership. Is that still the case?

*Jim*: Yes, I don't feel that I am getting the best out of my team really.

*Coach*: If you were getting the best out of them, what else would you be doing?

*Jim*: Umm. I'm not sure I know, really.

*Coach*: On what occasion in the past did you manage to get the best out of them?

*Jim*: Oh, they performed very well at the end of last year when all the changes were made in our department. They pulled together and everyone supported each other.

*Coach*: How did you manage them in that situation? (*Enabling him to see his strengths.*)

*Jim*: Well, I explained exactly what changes were being made and the whole team identified what they were willing to take on, in addition to their existing role.

*Coach*: So, you explained the changes and supported them to take on additional tasks (*paraphrasing*). Anything else?

*Jim*: Yes, we all worked on a new system to implement the changes that would work well for everyone.

*Coach*: I see. So a good deal of collaborative work to ensure the changes were implemented? (*Emphasising his strengths and creating trust.*)

*Jim:* Yes, umm that seems to be what is missing right now.

*Coach:* Say a bit more about that (*non-intrusive as he seems to have an idea*).

*Jim:* Well, I feel that currently the team isn't pulling together as they did. I have been very busy working on this new project and perhaps I haven't explained things as clearly as I might have. There are one or two new members of the team who haven't really been integrated as I would like.

*Coach:* It sounds as though you have a couple of ideas forming about explaining things clearly and integrating the new team members. What needs to happen now? (*Listening to his ideas and believing he has the answers, encouraging him.*)

*Jim:* Yes, I think I have been so tied up with this project that I have neglected the team over the past couple of months. I will arrange a team day away from the office to help integrate the new members and this will give me a chance to bring them all up to speed.

Not all coaching conversations will have the same results and, of course, some people may not be able to come up with the solutions for themselves. This may be for a variety of reasons. They may not want to change the situation or take ownership of a task. They may shy away from responsibility or new ways of thinking. As a coach, you will try to help your coachee find some way to progress. Small steps are often the way forward when staff are fearful of change or reluctant to accept new situations. You should pay close attention to interpret the true meaning or reasons behind the fears or reluctance. Your role is to probe and uncover the source rather than to fix the problem with a temporary plaster.

A coach once reported to me that the teams in their organisation were not pulling together: 'Following previous periods of instability and weak leadership, the team leaders are defensive and suspicious of change. The defensive tendencies lead to conflict between teams, lack of co-operation and a blame culture.' If coaching has been set up to address defensiveness and a suspicion of change, then naturally people will be cagey in the first coaching sessions, even if the sessions have been clearly explained and the agreements and boundaries of the coaching discussed openly. In such cases you should be patient and view the coachee as someone who has the ability to put aside their suspicions and defensive behaviour. Only if you really believe that the staff can change will the changes take place. What we intend to happen very often does.

What is going on in the following session (the second session of a programme of ten sessions)?

*Coach*: Morning, Sue, what would you like to use this session for today?

*Sue*: Well, I was thinking about the changes that are being made in the department, and really feel that I will never fit in. The way things are going, I can't see how I can possibly stay with the company (*slightly irritated tone of voice*).

*Coach*: What would need to happen for you to fit in do you think? (*Believing and communicating that the coach thinks she can fit in.*)

*Sue*: More than management are willing to do, that's for sure! (*She changes position and raises her eyes upwards.*)

*Coach*: Say a bit more about that, Sue (*allowing her to expand on what she said and probing deeper*).

Sue is feeling considerable fear here:

■ Fear of not fitting in.
■ Fear of losing her job.
■ Fear that the management will not support her.

As a coach, you need to remain detached and not allow yourself to be drawn in. As an internal coach, you may have great empathy with your coachee, but you should put aside any feelings you may have and support your coachee to trust the confidentiality of the session and to speak openly.

Sue goes on to describe at length how management has failed. She has had plenty of evidence to show that a blame culture exists and so she is naturally mistrustful and suspicious. The session continues:

*Coach*: Yes, Sue, I can sense your frustration. However, this coaching programme is now in place to enable us to move forward positively. If you were to get support from management, what specifically would you be looking for?

*Sue (long pause – no interruption from the coach)*. Umm, not sure. (*The coach is aware that Sue is still fearful of something and not able to voice her concerns.*)

*Coach*:You mentioned that the changes in your department meant you were finding it hard to fit in. What would enable you to fit in?

*Sue (another pause)*. Not sure I really want to actually... (*pause; coach stays quiet*). No, not sure at all (*pause*).

*Coach*: Not sure, Sue?

*Sue*: No, I don't feel at all sure about anything.

Here the coach could continue with the following questions:

- What would help you to feel sure?
- If you were sure, how would you be acting and feeling?

However, sometimes it is effective simply to state what is happening: to be totally honest with your coachee. After all, that is what you are aiming for – honesty and openness. The coach could then say, 'Sue, I am feeling a resistance here. I understand that you are unsure and that you want to fit in, but it seems as if we are not moving forward. What would help you here?' Very often the coachee will then begin to open up, particularly if the coach remains calm and believes in their coachee.

## STATING YOUR TRUTH

When people appear stuck, as a coach, you should retain your integrity by being honest about what emerges from the session. It is liberating for your coachee to hear what is happening because they are very often not able to see things objectively. You can then state clearly what you are observing, both physically and emotionally.

## USING BODY LANGUAGE

If your coachee waves their arm around in a circle, do the same and ask, '*What does this mean?*' (circling with your arm). If they point or indicate a place in the room, ask, '*What's over there?*' (pointing or indicating as they did).

Often just the knowledge that this is what they are doing can be very revealing to your coachee. It can open up a whole new area for getting to the heart of the issue (see also the section on 'Perceptual positions' in Chapter 7).

## LOOKING AT THINGS FROM A DIFFERENT PERSPECTIVE

Another method of helping your coachees to see beyond what is being communicated is to ask: 'Whom do you admire in this organisation? If you were to ask them about this issue, what would they say, do you think?' Sometimes taking the situation away from your coachee and allowing them to view it from a different perspective really helps to unblock them. Also, if someone is stuck and seemingly unable to move forward, try asking: 'OK, so right now this situation is preventing you from achieving your goal. Let's imagine you were out beyond this situation and the situation was behind you and dealt with. What would you be doing/saying differently?'

When you look at identifying the meaning behind the words therefore, there is a whole range of communication skills you can apply. You can:

■ use questions, reflect, reframe and summarise;

■ use pacing and mirroring;

■ help the coachee to hear what they are saying by paraphrasing what they are saying using their own words;

■ employ honest statements about what you see, hear and feel;

■ help your coachee to see what movements and body language they are using and the impact this may be having.

Naturally, there will be occasions where total honesty and reflecting feelings need to be modified. It is not always helpful for your coachees to hear you repeat how angry or ineffectual they are, even if they did say it themselves! In this case use your emotional intelligence to feed back in slightly modified language. Your aim is to remain positive and to allow your coachee to move away from negative emotions and feelings.

# 10

# Respecting others' worldviews and motivating your coachees

## BEING RESPECTFUL

You and your coachee's beliefs, attitudes, morals and values can affect the coaching process.

### Beliefs

**A belief** is something you accept as true. This may be an opinion you have gained from your own experience. For example:

- I believe that not all people are suited to a leadership role.
- Everyone should take action on global warming, no matter how small their contribution.
- I believe that cricket is the most complicated game ever invented.

### Attitudes

**An attitude** is a way of thinking or behaving. This is very often learnt behaviour or a way of thinking gained from experience. For example:

- Having a positive attitude is more helpful in life than being negative.

- I think it is important to look at all sides of the problem carefully before making a decision.
- Live for today!
- They only learn if I tell them again and again.

## Morals

**Morals** are an individual's sense of right and wrong. Some people are outraged when animals are killed for research; others feel that it is right to continue to discover valuable cures. This is very often a gut feeling that allows individuals to gauge when something is not 'right' for them. In coaching it is helpful to be aware that your coachees will not all have the same morals.

As a coach or mentor, blocks often arise during a session if your coachee is not morally aligned. If your coachee holds integrity as a high value and is required to be less than honest as part of their role, they will quickly become dissatisfied. If they are consistently told that their high moral stance is holding them back, they will become frustrated. Instead of 'telling' and making assumptions about who is right and wrong, therefore, try to understand how a situation has arisen. Ask open questions to discover what your *coachee* thinks they should do to get the result they are looking for.

## Values

Most businesses have a **values** statement. Some of the standard words that spring to mind are 'honesty', 'integrity', 'respect', 'inclusivity', 'high standards of customer care', 'environmentally friendly', 'flexible' and so on. Values guide our actions. They form our attitudes and influence our thoughts and expressions. Personal values can be fun, creativity, challenge, knowledge, achievement, peace, security, happiness, contribution and so on. For example, someone who values making a contribution may always stop to give small change to a homeless person in the street, whereas his partner may find this a waste of time and feel that saving the money towards a meal out is far more important.

## ACCEPTING DIFFERENCES

Even if we are not conscious of it, we are required to respond to situations and experiences every day based on our attitudes, morals, beliefs and values. If you are aware of how you have formed your own worldview, you will more easily accept the differences in those you are supporting through coaching and mentoring. It is important, therefore, to put aside (not abandon!) your own view of the world and to be open-minded when coachees come to sessions with beliefs, values and attitudes different from your own. Without this self-awareness, your sessions will not achieve the desired outcome.

Coaching anyone, no matter what their worldview, requires empathy. Empathy is seeing a situation though another person's eyes. It means standing in their shoes or sitting in their chair and feeling and thinking as they do.

### Exercise

*Christian was one of the directors of a large watchmakers in Zurich. He was very creative and had designed a revolutionary new watch aimed at the female market. He was ready to launch it and had taken the designs to a board meeting attended by four of the decision-makers. The following are the various reactions he received:*

1.    *Yes, the components are very easily manufactured and, in my opinion, it can be put into production right away, making it very cost-effective.*

2.    *This sits well on the wrist and is a beautiful addition to our range. It complements the men's watch we launched last year. I feel it is stunning piece that will enhance our reputation.*

3.    *Our customers will be delighted to know that we have come up with yet another great design. I can't wait to hear the reaction.*

4.    *Yes, I need to view the finished product and to be able to see what possible design modifications need to be made.*

*If you were coaching each of these individuals you would have greater success by approaching the sessions according to each's beliefs, attitudes and values:*

■    *Which of the statements above do you identify with?*
■    *What does this tell you about your own worldview?*
■    *What beliefs, attitudes and values are they expressing?*
■    *Are their attitudes wrong or just different?*

## MOTIVATING YOUR COACHEES

Each one of us is motivated by different things and, as a leader and coach, it is important to find out what motivates your coachees. It is also important to understand that what motivates someone may change, according to their circumstances. The most obvious way to find out what motivates your coachee is to ask them. Be curious about them, find out what they enjoy about their job, and if they have ideas or suggestions – you may be pleasantly surprised. If they are struggling, remain supportive and view them with a positive frame of mind. Ask them what it is that is bothering them and then listen carefully in order to understand. Take off your leader's hat, be a non-judgemental observer and see if you really can believe they have the answers because, very often, they have!

## Exercise

*Think of a challenging relationship you have with one of your coachees and then ask yourself the following questions:*

■ *How do I feel in their company?*
■ *On a scale of one to ten, how much do I respect them?*
■ *How far am I able to put any feelings or assumptions aside during sessions?*
■ *If I viewed them in a more positive light, what would I be thinking?*
■ *What do I need to do to remain objective?*
■ *How can I focus on their strengths?*

*If you want to build a relationship of trust and openness with your coachee, try the following:*

■ *Share a little of your own vulnerability with them.*
■ *Do not be afraid to share how you are feeling.*
■ *Notice what is going on in your mind during the session.*
■ *Reveal these thoughts if appropriate.*
■ *Ensure confidentiality at all times (unless otherwise agreed).*
■ *Keep to any commitments you make to your coachee.*
■ *Create a positive image of your coachee and focus on this during the sessions.*
■ *Use appreciative inquiry (see below).*

## APPRECIATIVE INQUIRY

When people are motivated, the way they behave and their

attitude to work is totally different from when they are not motivated. For several years I worked for Airbus as an executive coach where the challenge was to bring people together from different countries and cultures to form a single, European company. The stress and undeniably difficult circumstances surrounding this project made this a very daunting task, but there was not one coachee who was not highly motivated and thrilled at the prospect of being a part of this European project. It was this that made the difference to the success of the coaching programme.

In addition to a motivated workforce, the project manager's attitude was such that the strengths and individual performances of the company's executives were celebrated. The coaching programme was a reward for excellence and high achievement. This is the essence of appreciative inquiry.

Developed by David Cooperrider, appreciative inquiry is a method of coaching based on an individual's strengths, competencies and achievements. It focuses on what was happening when things were going well. In the case of Airbus, the focus was on how the various international teams worked well in the past: what key behaviours had produced results and what the most successful executives had done that worked. This enabled the coaching to focus on what might be achievable, challenging individuals to think outside their comfort zone and to create a clear vision for the future. Appreciative inquiry makes the assumption that focusing on the positive aspects draws people in, enabling them to work together more efficiently. It emphasises what works in the system and builds on those strengths to create positive change for the future.

## Exercise

*Use appreciative inquiry in your coaching sessions to boost your coachee's confidence. The questions you could ask include the following:*

■ *What are your key strengths?*

■ *What have been the most successful achievements you have made to date?*

■ *What happened that enabled you to be successful?*

■ *What did you feel/think at the time?*

■ *What key strengths did you drawn on for these achievements?*

■ *What can you do to build on these strengths for this project/situation?*

■ *What support do you need?*

*Reflecting on what your coachees say, you could then ask the following:*

■ *You mentioned x as a key strength. How can you build on that?*

■ *I noticed you were encouraged/motivated by x. How can you recreate that?*

■ *You were very positive when you described x. What can you do to rekindle that feeling in this situation?*

*When summarising, you could ask:*

■ *You mentioned how your confidence/motivation/enthusiasm around x has grown during this session. What will you do to build on this?*

■ *It appears that you are confident/focused/clear about this situation going forward. Is that correct?*

*If appropriate or useful you may add:*

■ *What will you now do differently?*

■ *What actions will you now take?*

■ *Who could support you in this?*

■ *What resources will you need?*

■ *How can I support you further?*

# 11

# Overcoming barriers to coaching and mentoring

## INDIVIDUAL BARRIERS

Despite good forward planning and clear guidelines to your staff about who or what is involved in the process, you will more than likely encounter individual barriers to coaching and mentoring. Individual barriers include the following:

- A lack of self-awareness.
- Unwillingness to change.
- Issues around confidence.
- Little knowledge of the process.
- Learning difficulties.
- Lack of support systems.
- Feeling there is no choice.
- A feeling that coaching/mentoring is just another 'tool'.
- Poor experiences of coaching/mentoring.
- No real belief that it can be effective.
- Cultural differences.
- Unresolved personal issues.

Just one, or several, of these barriers may be present, and there are a number of ways they can be addressed.

## Lacking self-awareness

A coachee's lack of self-awareness can sometimes be a daunting task for a mentor or coach to tackle, but it can often be addressed by incisive questioning and by challenging certain beliefs, often about other people. For example:

*Coachee:* My direct report, Anne, is a really difficult personality. She does a good job but no one really likes her and she can be so abrasive. Perhaps I should replace her.

*Coach:* You say that Anne is a difficult personality. Is that your opinion?

*Coachee:* Well, yes, she can be very confrontational.

*Coach:* Confrontational?

*Coachee:* Yes, she always goes against whatever I say.

*Coach:* So she challenges you?

*Coachee:* In a way, yes, but she doesn't want to listen to sense.

*Coach:* Sense?

*Coachee:* Yes, she can't seem to grasp my point of view.

*Coach:* So, what you are saying is that she goes against whatever you say, doesn't want to listen to sense and doesn't grasp your point of view?

*Coachee:* Yes.

*Coach:* Say a bit more about your point of view.

*Coachee*: Well, my point of view is usually the right one (*laughs as he says this*).

*Coach:* What made you laugh?

*Coachee:* Well, I suppose that sounds a bit arrogant, doesn't it?

*Coach:* Does it?

*Coachee:* Yes (*pauses*). Actually, Anne's ideas can sometimes be quite useful.

In this session the real breakthrough was when the coachee realised that his own way of being was arrogant. He was able to see that his attitude to Anne was part of the problem and, further on in the session, he began to see that a change in his behaviour could improve their relationship. As the coach reflected to him in his own words, he was able to hear what he was saying and notice the way he was coming across.

If people do not have any self-awareness (and you should be asking, 'In whose opinion?') and are really resistant or fearful, they may not respond to coaching at this time. They may identify mentoring or training as a way forward. Coaching in particular needs to be something your staff have chosen to engage in rather than it being forced upon them.

## Unwillingness to change

Sometimes carrying out 180° or 360° feedback* will enable people to see how they are perceived by others. This in itself can often lead to an individual recognising that they can develop and that they may need to change or modify some of their behaviour. As with a lack of self-awareness, it is important to realise that it may not be the best timing to coach or mentor everyone, but this does

---

* requesting specific feedback from a range of people connected to the coachee. For example, their boss, their peers, their secretary and so on.

not exclude it from being introduced at another point in their careers. Resistance to change can also stem from a fear of not being able to cope in a new role or system. This is where coaching and mentoring can achieve real transformation.

## Confidence

People often come to coaching and mentoring with beliefs that limit their progress. These may be long-standing voices in their heads or stories they have told themselves about their past or abilities. You can support your coachees to 'reframe' these beliefs and to view them as something they can choose to get rid of.

Persuading people to focus on their strengths by asking them to list their achievements can be revealing: people are often able to list their faults and development areas, but sometimes have difficulty listing their strengths. If your coachee is 'visual' they may like to fill in a SDOC (see Chapter 7). They will have areas of strengths even if these are not connected with their job role or work. The ERR model (see Chapter 6) may also help you when your coachee is caught up in the emotion of a situation.

## Knowing little of the process

Most people are familiar with mentoring: it has its roots in the old apprenticeship scheme that is now making a comeback. Anyone new to a role can be assigned a mentor to guide them and to give them advice when needed. If there is a specific skill one member of staff can offer others, they can be called upon to help and assist those who need to improve. IT skills, presentation skills, time management, knowledge of policies and procedures are all suited to mentoring.

People need to have information on the way both coaching and mentoring will be offered, with clear documentation and contracts in place (see Appendix 1 for examples). Ideally, a common information pack for coaching should be given out to potential coachees to prepare them for the sessions. Wheels, diagrams, goal sheets and any assessments must be made available to the coachees for study in advance of the sessions, where appropriate.

## Learning difficulties

Coaching and mentoring can be a vital support for those with such learning difficulties as dyslexia, hearing problems, impaired vision and so on. Often it is mentoring that is needed because people may need guidance and advice, particularly at the outset. It is also important for managers to recognise that everyone operates according to their own style. In a coaching or mentoring session, these styles can be explored and your staff can choose the best way for them.

In a large office run by a charity where the staff had a variety of learning difficulties, coaching and mentoring were offered and the staff were encouraged to share their time-management methods with each other. They were amazed by the diversity and range of systems used, from coloured filing systems to computer lists and wall charts. Through consultation, those with learning difficulties felt involved and were more accepting of the programme as a result.

## Lacking support systems

The staff in an organisation may feel they have no one to turn to in times of difficulty or change. No support systems may be in place such as regular appraisals, one-to-one sessions with a line manager, or clear lines of feedback and evaluation. Where staff development is supported by coaching and mentoring, clear communication channels and opportunities for feedback should be in place. All the staff who have signed up for the programme must feel supported and heard. Ideally, they should have access to an internal intranet, discussion groups and a range of websites and resources to support them in their development.

## Feeling there is no choice

Neither coaching nor mentoring will be well received if you do not give your staff an element of choice. People should be committed to the sessions and, ideally, they should have a choice of who is their coach or mentor: it has been shown that coaching, in particular, is more successful when the staff can choose their coach. This avoids possible personality clashes. In the case study described in Appendix 3, Kent County Council and Kent Fire Service trained a considerable number of their management staff to become coaches and mentors. As a result, all the trained coaches are able to coach in each other's organisations, and so all the staff are thus offered coaches from both organisations, allowing them a wide range of choice and personalities.

## Thinking that coaching or mentoring is just another 'tool'

Because mentoring has evolved from the old apprenticeship scheme, it is not considered unusual or a passing fad: most people are willing to be shown new methods or skills by a more experienced individual. Coaching, on the other hand, is often regarded as 'just another tool', and there may be some scepticism on behalf of management as to its value.

Coaching as a way of communicating is not new. Socrates wrote:

'I cannot teach anybody anything, I can only make them think.'

Since the first International Coaching Conference in Grindlewald in Switzerland in 2001, coaching has gained momentum. In the USA and Europe, most corporate and public organisations now train coaches internally or bring in coaching programmes and experts from outside, and the business case for coaching is well documented by the Chartered Institute of Personnel and Development (CIPD) in their *Guide to Coaching* (2004) If you are considering setting up coaching in your own organisation, the conditions are now more favourable than at any time in the past.

## Poor experiences of coaching or mentoring

You may have been assigned a mentor in your first job or a more experienced colleague may have just 'shown you the ropes'. Hopefully, this will have stayed with you as a positive memory. People can, however, have bad experiences that also stay with them and that affect the way they view being 'supported or helped'.

These memories may cause people to dismiss any kind of help in the future. One way of addressing these negative experiences is to allow such individuals access to colleagues who have had positive mentoring sessions. Positive messages about how mentoring has improved in recent years and real, tangible results can also help.

Coaching, on the other hand, may not be something everyone has had access to. Again, any positive sessions and/or outcomes can be discussed, in conjunction with case studies or experiences people may have had outside the organisation.

## Not believing that coaching or mentoring can be effective

As mentioned above, positive case studies and experience should serve to dispel any doubts. These days there is plenty of hard evidence available from the following coaching self-regulating bodies:

- The Association for Coaching (AC).
- The International Coaching Federation (ICF).
- The European Mentoring and Coaching Council (EMCC).

Additional resources include the Chartered Institute of Personnel and Development's magazine *Coaching at Work*, and the very informative *ReSource Magazine* that offers 'information about life enhancing change to the personal and business development world'. These magazines contain case studies and articles on both coaching and mentoring.

## Cultural differences

In a diverse workforce, it is essential to realise that cultural differences will play a part in both the perception of coaching and in the sessions themselves. In some eastern cultures, for example, it is not usual to share your thoughts and feelings with your work colleagues. In a coaching session, therefore, you may be met with blank stares and seemingly resistant body language.

Once again, it is important to be clear about what coaching and mentoring will address. You should explain in detail the way in which the sessions will be conducted and give specific guidelines and coaching demonstrations. This will help to dispel anxieties and fears about the process. As a leader, you will have to be patient and understanding if the sessions are slow to produce results. You should be flexible, adapt your style and ensure your staff are consulted and well prepared for the sessions.

## Unresolved personal issues

There will be times when coaching or mentoring will not be appropriate or useful. When people are struggling with personal issues (for example, financial difficulties or alcohol abuse), they will not react well to coaching or mentoring. In such cases, have a list of counsellors and/or therapists to hand and refer your coachee to someone who is qualified to deal with these issues.

Mentoring may be appropriate when the fears surround a certain skill or lack of knowledge. A more experienced colleague may be a welcome support and may be able to help individuals to gain valuable experience and to dispel their fears.

Coaching can support people who have problems with their self-esteem or feelings of frustration about work issues. However, it is vitally important to recognise when counselling or therapy is needed and to refer such people on. Trusting your intuition and setting clear boundaries around your coaching or mentoring role will ensure this happens.

## ORGANISATIONAL BARRIERS

There can be many organisational barriers to coaching and mentoring:

- Cost of training.
- Time (for sessions and cover).
- A lack of a buy-in from senior management.
- No real evidence of outcomes/impact.
- A culture where trust and openness are not encouraged.

- Poor systems and processes.
- Tensions and mistrust in the team.
- The perception of coaching and those being coached.

As with individual barriers, just one, or several, may be present, and there are a number of ways they can be addressed.

## Justifying the cost of training

Try to balance the cost of effective coach and/or mentor training against other interventions such as staff training, consultancy, tutoring, attendance at conferences, external qualifications and so on. Cost-benefit analyses have been carried out by many organisations proving that coaching and mentoring are very cost effective. You could also try running a pilot until clear outcomes and benefits are demonstrated (see Chapter 14).

## Justifying the time

Quality-focused thinking time can be very creative: it gives an individual the space to expand their thinking and can actually save time in the long run. It allows people to share their ideas, fears and difficulties in a confidential environment so that the process of change and/or acquiring new skills is less frightening.

## Overcoming a lack of buy-in from senior management

If you meet resistance from senior management, hold a meeting with all the stakeholders to demonstrate how coaching or mentoring can benefit your organisation. As with individual barriers, case studies are now freely available for discussion.

If you also develop a plan by setting out the scope, objectives, timescale and funding implications, this will serve to ease the process. Making sure that your objectives are in line with organisational goals and values will mean that you will have more chance of success (see the case studies in Appendix 3).

## Providing evidence of outcomes/impact

When you introduce coaching or mentoring, you should set up a monitoring and evaluation programme to ensure there are frequent reviews on how individuals are progressing. Some effective monitoring methods are as follows:

- Self-reflection on behalf of the coachee/mentee.
- How the coachee/mentee feels they are progressing with regard to personal and organisational goals.
- 360° feedback at the beginning and end of the programme.
- Staff surveys to measure behaviour changes and staff morale.
- External evaluation.

The benefits of mentoring are well documented, and it is now recognised that coaching can impact positively particularly on staff motivation and retention as well as contributing to increased productivity.

### Case study

*Newcastle City Council evaluated the benefits they experienced from training over 100 staff in Newcastle schools and colleges in coaching skills. The following are their conclusions:*

*'From the evaluation of our coaching training and from my personal experience I have noticed the following:*

- *Better teamwork and co-operation of staff*
- *Improved job satisfaction, morale and motivation*
- *Reduction in conflict and stress*

- *Improved self-management and achievement of targets and goals*
- *Increased success through more effective planning and prioritising*
- *More confidence and competence in a wider range of tasks and situations*
- *Better decision-making.*

I have recommended that we develop a structured programme of coaching over the next two years.' (Sue Blakemore, Newcastle City Council School Improvement Service).

## Encouraging trust and openness

Try to gain the trust of a few key people who will champion your cause. You may need to take small steps at first and start with one or two people who are willing to be trained as coaches.

### Case study

*In a UK manufacturing company where the culture was closed and mistrustful, four managers decided to set up an action-learning group to support each other. They asked me to facilitate the group, and I used coaching skills to enable these managers to bring up issues and challenges in a safe, confidential environment. They met once a month outside the office. After a period of six months they were able to facilitate the group themselves. Owing to the success of this group, they set up group coaching for their four departments. By the end of that year, they had successfully influenced senior management to take on one-to-one and group coaching in several areas of the company. They had demonstrated that open dialogue had increased trust and had changed the way people communicated.*

## Improving poor systems and processes

Most coaching and mentoring programmes need clear documentation and an effective system of delivery. Review any documentation and systems that are already in place to ensure these are effective. The following documents and processes should be in place:

- A clear contract to satisfy all stakeholders.
- A clear system of monitoring and review.
- The stated number, timing and frequency of the sessions.
- A statement where coaching or mentoring is clearly explained.
- A brief pre-session questionnaire.
- A review/self-reflection document.
- A document outlining the coaching tools and models.

## Addressing tensions and mistrust

Tensions and mistrust between team members can have a negative impact on coaching. One way to address this is to be as open and clear about the process as possible. If the documents and processes outlined above are all in place, much of this mistrust will be resolved. Emphasise the importance of confidentiality and record-keeping, and make sure your policies and procedures are inclusive and are worded sensitively.

## Changing the perception of coaching and of those being coached

While coaching can help people to find solutions to their problems, it is most often used to support people seeking:

- to manage change;
- promotion;
- a new role;
- clear decisions;
- effective delegation;
- ways to enhance team building;
- behaviour change;

■ clarity and focus;

■ new insights and ways of working; and

■ to motivate staff and improve performance.

If you encourage your staff to see coaching as a supportive and encouraging way of moving forward, you will have more success in promoting it.

## THE COACH'S OWN BARRIERS

As a leader/coach, you may have your own barriers to successful coaching: your previous experience may cause you to make assumptions, or you may fall easily into the trap of wanting to 'fix it' for your coachees. You may be sympathetic rather than empathetic and you may fall into colluding with your coachee in their 'story' or version of events. To overcome your own barriers, you could ask yourself the following questions:

■ How can I remain detached and accept this person as they are?

■ Can I accept that my coachee is OK where they are in this situation and just stay with that?

■ How can I give this person my unconditional positive attention?

■ What assumptions could I be making here?

■ To what extent do I think I could do a better job than my coachee?

■ If I want to 'fix it' for them or rescue them, how can I change my thinking?

■ Do I *really* believe that they have the answers that are the best for *them*?

■ Am I focusing on their strengths or their weaknesses?

■ If I have a tendency to collude with my coachee, what can I do to stay objective?

■ If I have an obvious solution to their problem, how can I focus on allowing them to explore alternative ways and remain detached from the outcome?

You may want to share your own expertise or ideas at the end of the session, but do so by acknowledging of your coachee's ideas: 'I agree that your idea looks sound, *and* (not "but") I'd like to let you know what I was thinking in case you'd like to consider my idea too.' Always keep in mind that people grow by trying ideas and methods for themselves. The ideas may not be the best ones, but people will learn and revise their decisions and enhance their experience as they go. This is only possible if you are able to stand back and let them!

# 12

# Understanding the role of power and authority

When you are coaching, you need to be aware of how you come across to others and you should not abuse your authority by allowing your knowledge of the individual and/or systems to influence your interventions.

## AVOIDING BEING AUTOCRATIC

The way you walk into a coaching session will have a great impact on the result of that session. If you have fostered an atmosphere of trust and openness you will be greeted in a different way from someone who walks into room wielding their perceived power and authority. Coaching is a conversation between equals.

## BRINGING ENERGY TO A SESSION

In supervision, I often find that coaches struggle with one specific aspect of their coachees' behaviour. They frequently say such things as 'She was very listless and appeared demotivated' or 'I wasn't able to get him to commit to any specific actions, even though he had identified them as important'.

On probing a little further, I often discover that the coach went into the session demotivated because of something that had happened just before. We are all human, and it is impossible for us to detach ourselves from our own feelings and emotions. However, we should be aware that the outcome of a session depends on the energy we bring to the room.

Imagine a time when you were at a conference or attending a meeting. Someone stood up and droned on in a boring dull voice, or lost the thread and appeared nervous. How did you feel? Bored, tired, a bit anxious for them? In other words, the speaker was evoking in you the same feelings as they were portraying! Now imagine someone who is motivated about their subject and speaks with enthusiasm and energy. How do you feel? Even if you are tired or have had a bad day, this speaker will be able to make you feel energised and motivated. In both cases you picked up on the energy field created in the room.

Notice the way the energy shifts in a meeting and how the atmosphere sways backwards and forwards according to the people and the situation. Also notice how you contribute to the overall feelings in the room: you may have habits you are not aware of and patterns of behaviour that are so familiar they have become ingrained.

## INCREASING YOUR AWARENESS OF YOUR OWN BEHAVIOUR

You do not have to change your personality, but, to increase your awareness of how you come across to others, you should know how your behaviour affects the outcome of a coaching session. Because you are coaching within the parameters of your organisation's goals, there will be times when you need to be more or less directive in your approach, but there are, nevertheless, certain factors that can undermine the coaching process and destroy the trust you have built up:

- Never manipulate the conversation or use leading questions to obtain the result you are looking for.
- Be on your guard against referring to issues outside the agreed boundaries of the coaching.
- Never show inappropriate emotion.

As a leader/coach, you may lose your balance from time to time. As long as you state clearly where you stand on the values, issues or decisions under consideration, however, you will not fall into the conflict and anxiety trap. There may also be occasions when you find yourself closing down when faced by coachees who appear to be resistant. *The only time this can really damage the coaching relationship is when you do not notice it is happening.* This is why coaching supervision is so important because it allows you time to reflect on your out-of-balance reactions (see Chapter 15). If you are able to raise your awareness and take responsibility for your moments of weakness, the quality of your coaching will improve significantly. If you continue to regard your coachee as having the ability to learn and grow and allow them to create their own plans, you should not misuse your leadership role and the perceived power and authority that go with it.

## ESTABLISHING THE BOUNDARIES

It is the boundaries set by the coaching contracts, agreements and policies that enable individuals to trust the coaching process. When clear contracts exist and when all the stakeholders are involved in the process, the issues around power and authority are greatly reduced (see Appendix 1).

## ALLOWING SPACE FOR IDEAS TO COME OUT

As a leader/coach, you do not need to know everything. In fact, if you are able to show your own vulnerability, this will greatly free up the sessions: it will allow others to be vulnerable and will create a greater rapport between you. Your staff will often come up with ideas and ways forward you may not have considered. This is exactly what leadership is about – allowing others to take over your 'manager' role and to support them in doing so.

If you are coaching in a situation where there is a lack of clarity or confusion, try sitting with that confusion for a while. It is often out of confusion that real ideas and changes emerge. State what you know and what you don't know, and be honest with your coachees. Deal quietly with your own anxieties and concerns and tolerate those of others. Allow your staff to delve deep into their inner wisdom and support them, to nurture their ideas. If they feel encouraged to explore and know that it is acceptable not to have solutions immediately, they will become more creative. As a leader/coach, you will be able to stand back from the process and allow your staff to take away their ideas and build on them.

# 13

# Setting up the first session

## PREPARING YOUR COACHEES

Coaching only works well when people are ready for it. People who volunteer for coaching should understand what is involved and be fully prepared. We have seen how important agreements and contracts are in this process. It is the content and clarity in these documents that will enable your coachees to trust the process. Ideally they should have been part of the discussion on what, if anything, is reported back from the coaching sessions.

### Introductory coaching session

Make sure you are not sitting in your usual position (in particular not behind your own desk as this will send the wrong message). Once you and your coachee are both comfortable, you can share with them the techniques you use to relax before a session. If they arrive rushed and seemingly stressed out, introduce some ways to create a relaxed atmosphere (breathing, stretching, getting a drink and so on). You can always walk outside and do the session there.

Explain that this process is to help your coachee feel heard and supported and that, as far as possible, you will put aside your role as their line manager/boss during the sessions. Ask them questions to find out if they are clear about the process, and find out if they have had any experience of coaching (or mentoring) in the past. Help them to understand that their own reflective time and pauses are important to their growth.

When you are coaching internally, be aware of positions of power: coaching should be a partnership of equals. Power can become an issue when a senior member of staff is coaching a subordinate. (This can also happen in reverse when a junior member of staff is coaching someone in a senior position.) You may therefore need to encourage a junior member of staff to disregard any previous knowledge or experiences they may have had of you as a senior member of staff before you begin to coach them. This will ensure the sessions are professional and effective.

In the introductory session, therefore, you should:

- make sure your coachee is fully aware of the purpose of coaching;
- explain your own role as a coach and how this will differ from your usual role;
- clarify your coachee's role, and outline what is expected of them;
- point out that there will be no advice or suggestions and that the coaching will focus on your coachee and their potential strengths;
- clarify how coaching can enhance those strengths and focus on further development;
- as far as possible, gain commitment and ownership of the process (see below);
- ensure the coaching agreements have been read and signed;
- create rapport by being genuinely interested in your coachee;

■ remind them that the responsibility for any outcome lies with them, while being supported by you and the organisation.

## Obtaining commitment

If someone really is going to do what they say and move forward with actions and changes, they will require the necessary skills and ability. If you are coaching someone in a senior position, however, it may not be necessary to elicit their exact actions with a timescale. Such a person should be perfectly capable of carrying out the actions they have identified.

Sometimes, however, it will be necessary to obtain the times and deadlines for actions so that your coachee feels a sense of responsibility. Again, your own sensitivity and your knowledge of the person will inform your decision about how much probing you should do to gain commitment from them. You can always check by saying: 'As I understand it, you will be doing $x$ and adapting $y$ by the end of the week. Is that correct?' Or 'OK, we are at the end of the session, so would you like to summarise the actions you will take/changes you are aiming for?' The latter places the ownership firmly on the coachee's shoulders and enables them to repeat what they have committed to.

Although you will not know whether they have stuck to their agreed actions, if you are an internal coach, your coachee will know your expectations. While looking over their shoulder would be totally unprofessional behaviour, there will be challenges when you are coaching as a line manager. In this situation you should be aware of the blurring of the edges between your role as coach and that of line manager. While this may not always work effectively (you are human, after all!), with practice it will become easier.

## CONFRONTING POOR BEHAVIOUR

Sometimes you will need to confront poor behaviour. For example, your coachee may:

- be late for coaching sessions;
- be inappropriately aggressive;
- lack respect for you;
- step over boundaries;
- not respect the terms of the contract; or
- be unethical, racist, homophobic and so on.

You will no doubt have come across such behaviour before as a leader in your workplace. In coaching, poor behaviour does not occur frequently, but it should be addressed immediately if it does:

- If possible, prepare well in advance.
- Write down the key facts and evidence before you confront your coachee.
- Get right to the point.
- Say what you have to say succinctly.
- Invite your coachee to join you in an adult discussion.

Open the conversation tactfully, bearing in mind the following points:

- Be brief and clear about your position and your feelings.
- Make sure your coachee understands and is clear about your thoughts.
- Find out in advance if others share your views.
- Plan, prepare and practise the start of your conversation beforehand.

- Be clear about how you hope to resolve the issue and your ideal outcome.
- Mention specific behaviours or situations you found unacceptable and give examples.
- Tell your coachee how you felt at the time.
- Make it clear what is needed to resolve the situation.
- Allow your coachee to give their side of the story and listen without interrupting.

Be assertive, but not aggressive, by standing your ground. At the same time, use positive language. This will temper any difficult feedback:

- Reflect or state specifically something the coachee has done well/effectively.
- State the facts or unacceptable behaviour as you see them, as briefly as possible.
- Invite a comment from your coachee.

It is always more effective to use 'I' rather than 'you' when dealing with tricky situations: 'you' can seem accusing. Compare the following examples:

- 'I am not prepared to accept this situation' *versus* 'You make this situation unacceptable'.
- 'I am very concerned about the way this has been portrayed' *versus* 'You have portrayed this badly and have made me very concerned'.

Always state your own feelings and thoughts about the situation using 'I' messages where possible. For example:

- 'This is the situation as I see/understand it' *versus* 'You obviously don't see/understand what I mean'.
- 'I don't share the same opinion and feel I am not being respected' *versus* 'Yes, that's your opinion but you are not respecting me'.

Using 'I' in these situations will enable your coachee to find a solution. If people feel accused they will be less likely to resolve the issue or to reach an agreement

## TONE OF VOICE AND INFLECTION

It is worth mentioning here that voice is a key element in successful coaching. The way your voice is heard when you ask a question, reflect thoughts and even give encouragement can vary greatly. If you are in any way insincere or less than genuine, this will show in your voice. You will no doubt remember many times when someone paid you a compliment and you knew full well that they were not sincere. Similarly, how many speeches have you listened to when you knew it was all 'hot air'? How did you know? By the tone and inflection of the speaker's voice, coupled with their body language.

Practise keeping your voice neutral without any edge to it or trace of judgement: 'So you feel that changing things around in the department would be beneficial, do you?' This question asked in a neutral tone with no stress on any particular words would be merely curious and interested. Asked in a sharper tone, perhaps with the stress on the first 'you', as if you feel this idea was less than helpful, would cause your coachee to clam up and feel judged.

If you really believe in your coachee's ability, if you honestly see their potential and if you genuinely want their success, your voice will not betray you.

# 14

# Presenting a business case for coaching

Before you present your case for the implementation of a coaching programme, you could ask yourself the following questions:

- Who will be involved in the programme?
- Who will the coaches be and who will be coached?
- How will the coaches be trained?
- If you change your role, how will you get people to accept you as their coach?
- How will you select your coaches?
- Will you draw on your staff's expertise or will you employ external coaches?
- What codes of practice will you work to?
- Who will be involved in drawing up the contracts and/or agreements?
- What should these agreements contain?
- What specific development and support needs will the coaching address?
- How can you ensure that coaching is seen as a positive way of moving forward, supporting and enhancing good practice?
- How will the effectiveness of the programme be evaluated?
- What support will your coaches receive in terms of supervision, resources and ongoing development?

You should also gather evidence to support the value of coaching programmes (Appendix 3 contains comments from participants on the Institute of Leadership and Management (ILM) Level 5 'Coaching and mentoring in management programmes' you may find useful here).

## ESTABLISHING THE OUTCOMES AND OBJECTIVES

To establish the programme's outcomes and objectives, in consultation with all the stakeholders, consider the following:

- Why does the organisation exist?
- What challenges does it face?
- What do you want to achieve with the coaching and within what timescale?
- How will you identify the development and support needs for all the stakeholders?
- What team/individual behaviours deliver the best results?
- How do you know?
- In what way will you measure the outcomes?
- How will the programme outcomes positively impact on other departments?

## RUNNING A PILOT PROGRAMME

Try to run a pilot programme to assess the cost effectiveness and benefits of coaching. In one organisation where four senior managers had trained as workplace coaches, a pilot coaching programme was run for 40 middle managers and team leaders. The aims were to reduce absence due to stress and to retain newly-trained managers who were feeling unsupported. The organisation set up a system where all four coaches posted their details on the intranet so that the participants could select their coach. The participants were all people who had responded to the request for 'anyone wanting to take advantage of confidential professional conversations to discuss workplace issues'. The coachees had six coaching sessions over a period of three months. As a result of this pilot, 50% of the participants cited coaching as a reason for staying in post. A further 30% said it had greatly reduced stress. At the end of that year, figures for absence due to stress-related illness had dropped significantly.

## A MODEL FOR PRESENTING A BUSINESS CASE

Figure 10 outlines a model that will help you to prepare a business case for coaching. This model comprises three sets of responsibilities. Your responsibilities for:

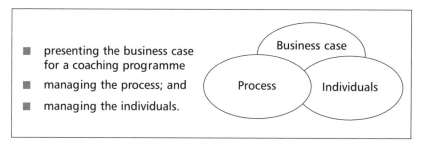

- presenting the business case for a coaching programme
- managing the process; and
- managing the individuals.

**Fig. 10. Preparing a business case.**

Your responsibilities for presenting the business case are as follows:

- Decide on the type of coaching for the programme (development, performance, career and so on).
- Identify the vision, purpose and aims of the programme.
- Identify the resources, people processes, coach training, systems and tools.

■ Create a plan to achieve the desired outcomes – deliverables, timescales and strategy.

■ Set up a cost analysis and budget for the training and the implementation of the programme.

■ Establish how the coaches and coachees will be selected.

■ Set standards, areas of confidentiality and quality control.

■ Demonstrate clearly how you will maintain overall performance and continuous professional development (CPD).

■ Set up reporting lines on progress to human resources/ leadership team.

■ Put measures in place for ongoing evaluation and review.

■ Discuss and delegate roles and responsibilities for the coaching systems and processes.

Your responsibilities for the process are as follows:

■ Agree and communicate the optimum standards of performance and behaviour.

■ Anticipate and resolve any barriers or resistance to coaching.

■ Communicate the benefits and tangible results coaching will provide.

■ Promote open discussion and agree where coaching will have the most impact.

■ Monitor and maintain an overview of the ethics and integrity, and maintain your focus on the objectives.

■ Set up clear timescales, session lengths and the duration of the programme.

■ Discuss suitable venues and cover for the sessions.

■ Develop and maintain coaching resources and networks.

■ Set up clear lines of reporting, ensuring confidentiality of the sessions.

- Identify individual responsibilities and administrative support.
- Facilitate and ensure effective internal and external communication.
- Give feedback on overall progress and coaching themes (if requested) to human resources.

Your responsibilities for each individual are as follows:

- Understand the coaches and coachees as individuals – personality, needs, values, skills, strengths, aims and fears – to find out what motivates them.
- Identify and initiate training for potential coaches.
- Communicate the benefits of coaching for CPD and support in times of change and growth.
- Enable and facilitate individuals to apply for coaching.
- Ensure individuals are able to meet and choose their coach where possible.
- Assist and support the coaches with problems, challenges and resources.
- Aim to establish coaching email links, groups and partnerships.
- Identify coaches' responsibilities and recording systems.

Additionally, you have responsibilities for the individuals being coached by ensuring that they:

- understand and are clear about the organisational and team goals;
- are committed to the overall vision;
- are prepared to align themselves with the goals identified;
- understand their part in the process and tasks.

## EVALUATING THE EFFECTIVENESS OF A COACHING PROGRAMME

For your pilot programme to demonstrate the benefits of coaching, you should establish quantifiable 'before' and 'after' criteria and ensure there is enough time between the 'before' and 'after' for change to be observed. In other words, you need to define what is to be measured by the pilot programme.

The 'before' criteria may be, for example, the number of hours wasted in:

- poorly prepared, unproductive meetings;
- communicating irrelevant information;
- doing tasks not part of the employee's remit/responsibilities;
- loss of production due to poor communication and a lack of essential leadership skills.

The amount of money so wasted is calculated as $x$ hours × an hourly rate (based perhaps on an average salary) $= A$. After coaching, the amount now lost is calculated in the same way $= B$. The cost of coaching ($C$) should be based, where possible, on at least two years $= C/2$. The equation, therefore, is $A - B + C/2 =$ (benefit).

Other criteria should be taken into account. For example:

- The general well-being of the manager.
- The level of motivation of the manager and members of the team.
- The retention rate.
- Creativity and innovation.
- Increased productivity.

These can be assessed through interviews, questionnaires and 360° feedback tools.

## IMPLEMENTING A COACHING PROGRAMME

The following case study concerns a large pharmaceutical company that wanted to set up a coaching programme to manage change:

### Case study

*One of the first considerations for me was the costs involved in implementing coaching initiatives, not least in terms of the time and effort of the people involved. I was, however, convinced that a coaching programme for our department was important as a method of supporting staff so that everyone felt easier about the changes taking place and could work out practical ways of organising and sustaining the process of planning the change.*

*I proposed that our department fund the coaching diploma for eight managers in my team. This would ensure that these members of staff had the appropriate training and coaching expertise.*

*The financial and time implications involved would be:*

- *£1,600 × 8 = £12,800.*
- *A minimum of 12 hours' coaching practice per manager (i.e. 8 × 12 = 96). This would entail managers being absent from work plus the time required to complete the coaching hours and course work.*

*All stakeholders agreed that coaching would enable managers to develop a positive approach to the proposed changes and the one-to-one sessions would be a safe confidential space to raise any concerns. It would serve to relieve stress and anxiety and focus on the opportunities opening up.*

*The trained coaches would need to put aside their own fears and coach others to be flexible and adaptable to cope with the proposed changes. Clear objectives for the programme were outlined, and we set up administration processes to manage the sessions properly and agree outcomes.*

*In order to function in the role of being a manager as a coach, they discussed how best to operate as a leader, offering support, effective feedback and encouragement, and staying detached as far as possible from the outcome of the sessions. They discussed the optimum behaviours that are important for making coaching work, such as listening, reflecting, delegating, motivating and so on. The coaches needed to be flexible because they manage a variety of individuals with different needs, styles and skill levels. The coaching course we selected from the Institute of Leadership and Management at Level 5 underpinned these skills. It also extended the emotional intelligence and essential communication skills of the eight senior managers.*

*Once the managers had been trained, coaching was set up on a two-weekly basis over the next six months. This resulted in more effective leadership and improved confidence. We noticed that managers were more motivated, leading to improvements in the performance of their individual team members. They were able to see that change can provide opportunities and enhance behaviours despite the initial extra work needed.*

*If a coaching programme is set up with clear guidelines, boundaries and evaluation, the benefits can be significant. Managers told us that they were motivated by the organisation being prepared to invest in time and support for them. This led to greater employee engagement, better working relationships and a more positive attitude towards development and change.*

*The coaching programme was evaluated with regular monitoring and review with managers and senior managers on an informal basis, and during regular meetings both with the team and one to one with the coachees. They were also asked to complete a questionnaire which they had devised with their coaches.*

*Follow-up meetings were set up to check progress. This enabled me, as the coaching programme co-ordinator, to stay in contact with both the coaches and the team members to show my commitment to the programme.*

# 15

# Supervision and coaching super-vision

Supervision is a word that is often associated with someone 'looking over your shoulder'. However, in coaching it is an essential way of keeping people safe and continuously developing. Some coaches therefore separate the 'super' from the 'vision' and call it 'super-vision' to make this distinction clear. As a coach who uses David Grove's 'clean language' during coaching sessions (see Chapter 7), I prefer to call the super-vision I carry out 'clean vision'. The SUSTAIN model outlined later in this chapter demonstrates what clean vision sets out to achieve.

## SUPER-VISING

To explain how super-vision can support coaches in the workplace, I interviewed the founder of the CSA Coaching Supervision Academy, Edna Murdoch, who is one of the world leaders in coaching super-vision.

**Q. How can super-vision support internal coaches?**

**A.** Super-vision helps coaches to think about the organisation they are working in and how the organisation's values impinge on their work and the person they are working with. It's about aligning the coach's, the coachee's and the organisation's values. Super-vision is about looking at those tricky conversations that coaches may need to have with the line manager or any of the stakeholders in the coaching process. Those conversations are tricky because internal coaches are very often looking over their shoulder. They do not have the freedom that external coaches have. They have to deal with setting boundaries within the organisation and with ensuring confidentiality. Coaching is surprising. Sometimes things are said or facts/information emerge in a coaching session which are really uncomfortable for a coach to know about. Coaches then have a piece of information that lies heavily with them. In a conversation with a supervisor they can figure out what to do with that information. For example, they may learn some personal information about a coachee that may impact or prejudice another piece of work they are doing within that department.

**Q. What are the benefits of engaging a super-visor?**

**A.** A super-visor brings a lot more training and understanding of the intricacies and relationships involved. The super-visor's work is supported by their knowledge of psychology and an understanding of systemics. In other words what goes on in organisations and how the different parts relate to each other. They are qualified to support someone to clarify their own understanding of those sometimes very complex contexts. They may also choose to use the seven-eyed model to explore complex issues. This provides the coach with a map/model or system to help clarify and understand the dynamics.

**Q. What is the seven-eyed model?**

**A.** This... model [was] developed by Peter Hawkins and it has seven eyes that is – seven ways of looking, a *super*vision of what's going on. It explores what is going on right inside the coach as they work. It explores what is going on between the coach and the person they are working with, and potentially what's happening inside the coachee. The model will also look at what's going on in the organisation and how that has an impact on the process. That can then be fed back into the super-vision. It's about illumination so that the coach goes away with a clear 'super' vision of their practice. Super-visors are trained to hold and explore a lot of conversations simultaneously.

**Q. How does super-vision differ from normal coaching interventions?**

**A.** I think that holding all those different conversations and relationships at the same time is one of the major differences. Also when you use something like the seven-eyed model you are looking at a range of different perspectives – for example, what is going on in the organisation to what is happening with the coach...Super-vision ensures that the coaching is strong, true and uninhibited and the coach is comfortable with talking to the organisation to enhance coaching...

The super-visor will support the coach in developing his/her own internal super-visor and so become more aware cognitively, somatically and intuitively as they work. This helps them to be aware of the hunches and intuitive glimpses and to be able to work with them in the moment, guiding truly effective interventions. It's the ability to use all this fine material as they are working with someone that signifies powerful coaching. As coaches develop this internal super-visor it will become something that they will listen to much more to support their interventions as a coach.

The main benefits of having a coaching super-visor, therefore, are that you:

- create safety for yourself and your coachees;
- develop your own mindfulness and intuition;
- grow in knowledge, skills and application;
- increase your self-awareness and sensitivity;
- see issues and situations from another perspective; and
- enhance your own coaching interventions and awareness.

Coaching super-visors should have the following:

- A knowledge of coaching and of super-vision.
- Familiarity with working in organisations.
- A high level of emotional intelligence.
- An ability to deal with resistance and negative attitudes.
- An ability to negotiate with all the stakeholders with tact and diplomacy.
- Familiarity with the existing systems but the ability to detach from them.

Above all, coaching super-visors should support their supervisees and the organisation but without colluding with them. Only in this way will super-vision be successful and enhance the development of coaches and leaders in the workplace.

## THE SUSTAIN MODEL

SUSTAIN is a model of coaching supervision: **S**ituation/issue, **U**nderstanding and context, **S**upportive relationship, **T**ools and systems, **A**wareness/presence, **I**nsights/learning and **N**urturing/ sustaining.

As a coach super-visor, you sustain your supervisees and the organisation in which you work:

- Supervisors have a clear overview of the Situation and clarity around issues.
- They foster Understanding and explore the context and background.
- This helps to create a confidential and Supportive relationship.
- They investigate patterns and share knowledge of Tools and systems.
- In building Awareness they create an energetic presence where ideas flow freely.
- This enables Insights and encourages learning.
- By Nurturing and supporting they sustain growth and ensure safety for their supervisee, client and organisation.

## THE CIRCLE MODEL

I have developed the circle model specifically for internal coach super-visors and for those working for several months in an organisation (see Figure 11). When you work in an organisation of any size, it is vital that you first make sure clear contracting is in place. It may also be necessary to re-contract at any point in the process if need be. This will ensure the coaching is addressing both the requirements of the company and those of the coachee.

## Contracting

What is to be reported in the super-vision should be clearly stated at the outset and a contract signed by all parties. The super-visor should oversee the process and ensure clarity and safety for all concerned. This happens best when there is frank and open discussion and where everyone's needs are respected.

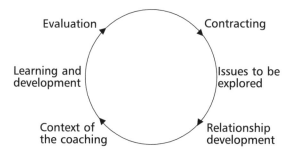

**Fig. 11. The circle model.**

# Exploring the Issues

After contracting, the super-visor and coaches explore the issues the company and the coachee have identified as the agreed areas for coaching. It is important to ensure that the company and coachee goals are in alignment and that this is an open discussion for all the stakeholders. It must be understood by all concerned that the actual coaching sessions are confidential but that there will be some reporting if required.

# Developing the Relationship

If the above guidelines are followed, this will pave the way for a relationship built on respect, trust and openness. In this phase there is mutual assessment to see if the coaching partnerships are the right fit. The clearer the contracts and agreements, the more trust individuals will have in the process. They will be happy to share their successes and concerns in this confidential setting.

# Coaching Context

The next step is for the coach super-visor to clarify the coaching context and the systems that are currently operating in the workplace. This is where all the stakeholders have an open discussion on the key areas for coaching. The coachee should be encouraged to align these areas with the key business results that have been discussed. It would also be beneficial for them to identify specific leadership behaviours to optimise these results.

## Learning and development

Together with the coach, the coachee develops an action plan so that they can explore the areas where they would like to learn and develop. The coach super-visor encourages the coach to reflect on and challenge their beliefs and assumptions.

## Evaluating

Both half-way through and at the end of the agreed number of coaching sessions there is some form of evaluation. The coach, the line manager or human resources can carry this out. The coach super-visor supports the coach in this evaluation process and maintains effective channels of communication with all the parties. Evaluation may take the form of an open discussion, 360° feedback or a questionnaire. Once again the agreement of all the stakeholders is crucial to the success of the coaching programme.

## SELF-SUPER-VISION

The questions and interventions below are aimed at the individual coach or mentor. However, the rewards to the organisation from having an effective method of 'self-super-vision' are great. One method is the double-loop learning concept developed by Argyris and Schön (1978). In single-loop learning, actions are often repeated without question or dialogue in order to achieve the same outcome. In double-loop learning on the other hand, assumptions are challenged, new systems devised and strategies re-thought to improve performance.

## DEVELOPING YOUR OWN INTERNAL SUPER-VISOR

All coaches and mentors are advised to analyse why they use a particular intervention or ask a specific question. As a result of so doing, over time you will develop your own internal super-visor. The questions you should ask yourself to develop your own internal super-visor are as follows.

*Before the session:*

- What do I need to do/think/change in order to believe in my coachees unconditionally?
- How can I gain a greater insight into what is happening for this coachee?
- What am I expecting from myself in this session?
- What do I want for myself and why do I want it?
- What do I expect from my coachees?
- Are my expectations justified?
- What do I want for my coachees and why do I want it?
- Could I challenge them more?
- Is there total trust and safety in this relationship so that I can challenge them?
- If not, how can I ensure trust and safety in the sessions?
- What can I do/think/feel so that this session is given the best chance possible?

*After the session:*

- Was I being totally non-judgemental?
- Did I believe in my coachee's qualities and knowledge?
- What did I *expect* them to do or say?
- What did I *want* them to do or say?

- What could I have done or said that would have helped them to move forward?
- What interventions can I make to reveal how they feel about the actions they have agreed to?
- What was my reaction to their response?
- Why did I react in that way?
- What feelings were evoked in me?
- What do those feelings mean in this context?
- What assumptions was I making?
- What impact did these assumptions have?
- Was I judging? If so, to what extent?
- Was I believing in my coachee's potential?
- What needs to happen next for my own growth?

By answering the above questions you will notice that your personality forms part of who you are as a super-visor. This will influence how you show up to the sessions and the way you react to the coach and their situation. Some further questions you may like to ask yourself, therefore, are as follows:

- If my supervisee wants advice, do I give it freely or do I encourage independent thinking?
- If I find that my supervisee is crossing the accepted boundaries, how do I handle this?
- My supervisee is having a real moan and feeling a victim. Do I collude with them?
- The contracting for this piece of work looks shaky. Do I challenge the coach or let it rest?
- My gut feeling is that the organisation is not supporting the coaches. Do I have the courage to address this?

In answering these kind of questions you will become aware of your own feelings and behaviours. You will also be able to tell where you have acquired certain patterns of behaviour such as colluding and avoidance. You should modify these if necessary and seek help if appropriate.

# 16

# Co-coaching and team coaching

## CO-COACHING

Co-coaching (or peer coaching) involves one coach practising their coaching skills on another coach, and this is often used in staff development. For example, peer-coaching groups have long been employed to support school improvement plans, and the reported benefits of this have included teachers developing the capacity to be more reflective and being able to explore what impact their behaviour had on their students' learning and how to address this. In some schools, the teachers pass their coaching skills on to their pupils so that sixth formers, for example, can support younger pupils with both coaching and mentoring as well as co-coaching each other.

If you intend to set up a co-coaching programme in your own organisation, there are certain conditions you should first ensure are in place:

- The coaches should be trained to a high standard by a recognised coach training organisation (see below for some suggested training exercises to get you started).
- There should be an atmosphere of trust and openness.
- All the staff should be encouraged to foster strong relationships.

■ There should be a cohesive organisational culture that enables effective decision-making and collaboration.

Coaches who have also co-coached have reported the following benefits of co-coaching:

■ An increased retention of new systems and strategies.
■ An ability to apply new techniques and skills more effectively than before.
■ The ability to give neutral observations and non-judgemental feedback.
■ Better relationships with their peers.
■ New respect and trust.

## TEAM OR GROUP COACHING

Two of the biggest barriers to introducing a coaching programme are a lack of time and money. One solution is to set up group coaching for teams or individuals who have the same objectives. During these sessions, the coach asks some incisive questions to encourage the team to broaden their thinking or to look at things from another point of view:

■ What makes you think that is the best solution? (Keep your tone neutral.)
■ What else have you considered?
■ What assumptions could you be making?
■ What would be the consequences of this action?
■ What if...?'

As a team coach, you should know when it is appropriate to intervene in a discussion and when to let it ride. The intention is not to make a decision for the team but to facilitate their thinking – to ensure they listen to each other and sensitively feed back ideas and solutions that have been put forward. This is why coach training is so essential for team coaching: as a team coach, you should be skilled in using your intuition and judgement and the appropriate interventions.

The teams should also be prepared for the new way of working. They may not be familiar with deep listening, giving feedback to colleagues and clear decision-making. They may be daunted by the added responsibility and perceived ownership of unfamiliar tasks. As the coach, you should ensure that the team is equipped with the skills and resources they need to self-manage. You should anticipate and deal with problems, monitor progress and provide ongoing support. This may involve:

■ setting up clear processes and reporting lines;
■ allocating team leaders;
■ assigning tasks and identifying team roles;
■ identifying key skills and knowledge gaps;
■ setting up training where necessary;
■ monitoring the progress of tasks and projects; and
■ discussing failures and celebrating success.

The time spent in team or group coaching sessions is more than recouped by the improved efficiency and effectiveness of the individuals being coached.

## Co-COACHING AND TEAM COACHING: EXERCISES

### Using 'what' questions

This is an exercise you could employ early in the training programme. The coach can ask questions beginning 'What' or 'What else...' only. They should offer no advice or suggestions.

The first question is: 'What would you like to use this session for?' The final question can be: 'What needs to happen now?', 'How can you take this forward?' or 'What one action can you take that would move this forward?'

Divide your group into triads. One person is the coach, one the coachee and one the observer. The coachee then chooses a topic they would like to work on (for example, time management, effective delegation, task organisation, taking on a new role, preparing for an interview and so on). They next outline the situation briefly to the coach and respond to their questions. At the end of the session the coachee feeds back to the coach what questions they found particularly helpful and which not so helpful.

The observer listens and observes the body language of both the coach and the coachee. At the end of the session they feed back the following comments with no judgements attached to them – these comments are not concerned with the *content*, only with the process:

- I noticed that *x* question was effective because...
- I observed that...
- I found *x* or *y* interesting because...

## Showing the differences between 'Yes, but' and 'Yes, and'

Set up groups of three to six people. Each person puts forward an idea (for example, 'I think we should have a new system of communication'). The next person continues with 'Yes, but'. Keep going until all the members in a group have come up with an idea. People may now be feeling frustrated because 'but' is usually followed by a negative comment or observation. The same activity is repeated but this time the second person says, 'Yes, and . . .' See how much freer and more positive the second round is!

## Team-coaching exercise

I carry a little bag of various small objects when I am coaching as I find this is a useful resource. It helps people to 'see' and 'feel' what is often stuck in their minds or jumbled in their thoughts. Spread 20 or so of these small objects (finger puppets, a tiny clock, a small pencil sharpener, a key, coloured stones, pieces of Lego and so on) on a table and ask the team to pick an object they can identify with. Ask each of them to place themselves on the table in a position that represents where they are in the company (the centre is the hub). Next, ask if everyone is happy about where they are or if they want to change their position. Allow them to talk and move around the table. Then ask the following questions and request that they just think about their answers as you pose the questions:

- If you could change where you were on the table, where would you be?
- What has prompted this idea to change?
- If you could change the positions of others, where would they be?
- What has prompted this desire to change their places?
- What would need to happen for you to be in your chosen place?
- If you are in your chosen place, how do you want things to move forward?
- Now the team is positioned, what needs to happen?
- What actions do you need to take?
- What else?

Then open up the table for discussion. Allow the team to ask each other the same questions. As the trained/experienced coach, you should facilitate this discussion. Reflect what you hear but with no judgement:

- I notice that...
- I realised that...
- I felt that...
- What was interesting was...
- I found *x* very revealing.

Stick to the facts and allow the comments to flow easily.

## Group hot-seat coaching

For this exercise, the coachees sit in a circle around an experienced coach in the 'hot seat'. The experienced coach asks if anyone would like to suggest an issue or challenge to be coached on. The volunteer coachee is then coached by the experienced coach. The other participants then offer observations (not advice or suggestions) on the coaching (not on the content) (for example, 'I saw that...', 'I noticed that...', 'It was interesting to understand that...').

The participants are next asked if they would like to coach someone, and a volunteer is asked to come forward as the coachee. If no one volunteers, the experienced coach continues to coach volunteer coachees with other issues or suggests an issue for people to coach in triads.

## Triad coaching activity

For this exercise, one person is the coach, one person is the coachee and one person is the observer. The observer can only comment on the coaching interventions and give encouragement and supportive feedback. They should avoid offering advice. They should tell the coach what they heard/felt/noticed, the impact this had and how this effected a change or development. For example:

■ I noticed that your second question made the coachee really think before replying. This showed to me that it made her think more deeply.

■ After you reflected what the coachee had said, I noticed that he seemed much lighter and his mood changed. He was obviously encouraged by hearing what he had achieved.

The experienced coach listens in and gives feedback to the group when the sessions are finished. Ideally, the coachees should bring their own projects, challenges and issues for coaching.

*Note*: This exercise can also be used for coaching super-vision as more experienced coaches can bring the issues they have had with their own coachees to the triad. This helps them to develop their techniques and lines of questioning and to obtain support and advice.

## Being totally focused in a session

This works best in groups of four to six people. Give each group a ball and ask them to throw the ball to each other in a circle. Ask them to notice how they are focused on the ball and where it is coming from. Give the groups another ball so that each group now has two balls. Ask them to throw the balls as before around the circle.

As this activity becomes faster, the concentration increases. Ask the group to notice that every other thought in their heads is sidelined when they are focused on the ball-throwing. This is the kind of focus coaches need in their coaching sessions.

# 17

# Organisational approaches to coaching

*Developing Coaching Capability in Organisations* is a report published in 2007 by the Chartered Institute of Personal Development (CIPD) in conjunction with Ashridge Centre for Coaching. It found that there are three broad organisational approaches to coaching:

■ Centralised and structured.
■ Organic and emergent.
■ Tailored middle ground.

## CENTRALISED AND STRUCTURED

Centralised and structured processes are evident in the BBC, where 80 trained coaches now run regular sessions. Issues of power and authority are addressed in the coaching programme through training, continuing professional development and regular coaching supervision. The following extracts are from an interview I conducted with Liz Macann, Head of Executive, Leadership and Management Coaching, who introduced the coaching programmes at the BBC.

**Q. What prompted you to set up the coaching programmes in the first instance?**

**A.** A colleague in Training and Development advertised a pilot coaching scheme on the internal intranet. She asked people to respond if they would like the opportunity to think through their own personal work-related issues in a confidential space. She was inundated with requests and from this pilot grew the understanding that there was a gap to plug. I then developed this idea as a consultancy project and believed that the coach practitioners would need to be really skilled for it to work and, as I passionately wanted coaching to take off, I decided that to begin with, at least a dozen people would need to be properly trained as coaches.

Of course in 2001, there were not the books or courses available that there are now, so we really had to invent our own wheels which we did by asking ourselves what training would *we* like to have had, what conditions would *we* like to have present if we were being coached and so on. In true coaching fashion, we started with the end in mind! So we set about creating a coaching programme to work on business objectives which developed gradually into the whole portfolio and infrastructure that we have today.

**Q. What has coaching had the most impact on?**
The BBC invests heavily in leadership development and one-to-one coaching is seen as the glue which makes the training stick. We have also seen a big shift in the way people who have been coached approach their problems and the way they manage other people, which in turn passes on that way of working to others. Many of the requests for coaching are around enhancing leadership skills and behaviours.

We may bring in external coaches to work with staff on things such as high-end strategy or corporate-wide sensitive issues, as we feel they are better placed to do that.

**Q. Do you think coaching programmes can be introduced by middle management or is it essential for top management to buy into the process?**

You can start in a small way and it will grow, because it works. This is not just something I do, it's something I completely believe in. If you are doing it with best practice and true integrity, and have people coaching who really believe in what they are doing, it will expand – it just will. Yes, it's great if all the senior management team buy in to the concept and it cascades down but that's not how we started. We began in the middle level, in a small way with the pilot programmes and it just grew.

**Q. What are the advantages of having trained internal coaches as apposed to external?**

Well, it's a *lot* cheaper and, if properly trained, they are a fantastic resource. You could say they are part of the same culture and so are 'bringing stuff' to the sessions and could collude, but we don't find that. Clients say that they like having someone who recognises the climate that's around in the BBC. I believe that the provision needs to be run as professionally as a private coaching company, so we make sure that our own coaches are receiving monthly supervision and professional development as well as backing the programmes up with efficient administration.

It's a huge co-ordinated operation now. At any one time we have between 70 and 80 trained internal coaches and we have a process for engaging external coaches if required.

It is interesting that as well as clients reporting that coaching helps them to be more effective and happier in their jobs, the coaches at the BBC say that one of the reasons they stay with the organisation is because of the coaching they do.

So we are successfully retaining some of our top people in more than one way! We also hold the view that if people leave as a result of the coaching, that is a positive too. If coaching can clarify their thinking and allow them to see that this is completely the wrong place for them, it's not what they want to do – then this is better for everyone. So the positive results are not always obvious.

**Q. How have you evaluated the results of coaching?**
The BBC's bottom line is the audience, and to get a measure on how coaching affects that is impossible. But we evaluate each programme and the coach's performance and find out the level of effectiveness of each programme. We do this from the manager's, client's and coach's point of view, to measure against the set objectives that were agreed in the three-way meeting at the beginning. The staff surveys show a huge increase in satisfaction levels and the feedback collected shows to what extent the teams are working more collaboratively, managers are managing better and so on.

**Q. How has coaching and being involved in this development within the BBC affected you personally?**
**A.** Oh it's completed changed me. I totally believe in the concept of 'unconditional positive regard'. I am far less judgemental than I was, and I rarely give advice, as I believe that you can't give people answers to their problems, as no-one knows all of the component parts of an issue except the individual themselves.

## ORGANIC AND EMERGENT

The second approach identified in the CIPD report was organic and emergent. Here coaching is used for different purposes and in a variety of situations. In education, for example, it is employed for performance management, classroom observation, one-to-one conversations for continuing professional development (CPD) and for meetings with parents. In the following case study, once again, qualified external coaches were hired to train key members of staff over a period of eight months.

## Case study

*We now have an in-house team of six people trained as coaches. The one-to-one coaching support has been promoted to all staff via a leaflet, but word-of-mouth has more impact and that is happening now.*

*Impact of the coaching programme:*

- *The development of middle leaders in the school. It is part of our CPD programme for Heads of Department, where they are initially trained in some of the basic techniques to use with their staff and also receive some personal coaching themselves. It is also part of the programme for those on the NCSL (National College for School Leadership) 'Leading from the middle' course.*
- *Support staff have received some one-to-one coaching as well.*
- *We now have staff requesting coaching, particularly those new in posts of responsibility and those new to the school. This support is very welcome.*

*Behaviours/attitudes/situations covered in the coaching sessions:*

- *Skills of leadership/handling staff.*
- *Confidence for those in new roles – a support, especially for NQTs (newly qualified teachers) (we may make this a compulsory element of their NQT year next year).*
- *Willingness to try different techniques to help the students learn in the classroom; to hook the learner rather than focusing on behaviour for some teachers.*

■ *Willingness to be more open and share issues with someone else – much more healthy.*

*Evidence*

■ *Feedback from staff involved – they especially like having time to think things through.*

■ *Observing some coaching skills being used around the school.*

*This is still early days but I feel it is beginning to have a positive impact!*

(Helen Pringle, Assistant Head, Walbottle Campus, Newcastle upon Tyne).

## TAILORED MIDDLE GROUND

The third approach identified by the CIPD was the tailored middle ground – a combination of the two approaches exemplified in the case studies.

### Case study

*Newcastle upon Tyne local authority (delivered) several 'Introduction to coaching skills' two-day courses to a wide variety of education providers . . . In the case of Gosforth High School, four teachers participated, after which they all chose to progress to the Certified ILM Level 3 Certificate in Coaching.*

*To establish a coaching culture in the school we adopted a two-pronged approach: an external coach to provide individual leadership coaching to members of the senior management team and the four ILM trainee coaches offered coaching to any interested staff . . . At this stage, a small number of specific people were targeted by the Head of HR to be coached in order to deal with certain problems.*

*A more organised and structured approach was adopted from September 2007... The original offer of in-school coaching for any interested person remained but in addition all heads of subject were offered at least two coaching sessions over the year... Some of these heads of subject opted for more than the two sessions as they found it so useful. Crucially, coaching sessions could be counted as part of the twelve hours of continuing professional development (CPD) which all staff were obliged to do. From May 2008 it was decided that six coaching sessions would be part of the induction programme for new managers, both those coming from outside the school and those who had been promoted internally.*

*The results have all been very positive in various ways. Everybody appreciates coaching for simply being a chance to be listened to and valued, but I would say all our coachees have gained something specific too in terms of problems being solved or sorted. As part of the induction process it's a bit too early to say, but again it's positive. We will be monitoring it more carefully after two terms.*

(Sarah Fearon, Head of History, Gosforth High School,
Newcastle upon Tyne)

---

(More case studies can be found in Appendix 3.)

# Appendix 1

# Sample forms and competences

## THE COACHING AGREEMENT

### Sample 1

#### *The purpose of a coaching agreement*

This coaching agreement aims to set out clear definitions and expectations from both the coach and coachee prior to any coaching sessions taking place so that both parties are aware of their individual responsibilities which foster an effective coaching relationship. This coaching agreement is intended as a guide and may, if necessary, be renegotiated by the coach during the course of the coaching relationship if in the best interests of the coachee.

Coaching works well when you:

- Are open and willing to consider change where this is necessary to aid development.
- Are open to new ways of learning and working which might challenge your thoughts and ideas.
- Are honest with your coach and yourself, particularly if you do not feel that something is working for you.
- Are ready to commit to your development by the giving and receiving of honest feedback.

- Recognise the investment being made in your development.
- Accept that commitment must first come from you before you can reap the benefits.

As your coach, I will endeavour to:

- Be focused on you and your best interests, which include your goals and your outcomes.
- Support and encourage you while you develop to your full potential.
- Be open, objective and non-judgemental, enabling you to set and work towards your own goals and achievements.
- Ask you questions that might challenge your ideas and thoughts as you progress and develop.
- Arrange a comfortable, private venue for our face-to-face discussions.

## *Confidentiality*

As a coach, I will observe confidentiality at all times, including the content and nature of our discussions, as this builds mutual trust and rapport. This rule of confidentiality, however, may be compromised if there is risk or potential risk, as follows:

- Where there is unacceptable risk to people and/or services.
- Where there is a breach, or potential breach, of law or contract.
- Where the organisation's policies and procedures are put at risk or potential risk.
- Where the coach and coachee agree that the issues raised cannot be appropriately managed or dealt with through a coaching relationship.

■ If the coach feels that the coachee's progress needs to be discussed with their line manager, which would be agreed prior to any sessions with the coachee.

As a coachee, however, you may decide that you wish to share your experiences with others, if you feel this is appropriate. It is important to remember, however, that your experiences are personal to you, and you should consider the impact your values and beliefs may have on others by the sharing of such information.

### Feedback

Every couple of coaching sessions you will be provided with a feedback sheet which I will ask you to complete, to ensure that the coaching sessions continue to meet your needs. This is your opportunity to be honest about how you feel the sessions are assisting you to reach your goals and outcomes.

### Records

I confirm that all records and feedback sheets will be kept confidential and secure during the course of the coaching sessions and that, at the end of the coaching relationship, these records will be destroyed confidentially.

### Cancellation

In the event you wish to change the coaching session, for whatever reason, I request at least 24 hours' notice (except in an emergency) and, unless you have notified me otherwise, I will assume you will be attending the session.

This coaching agreement is not an open-ended contract and I propose that the number of sessions offered will initially be six, of 90 minutes each, although this will be assessed and renegotiated, as appropriate, throughout the coaching relationship and depending on your goals and outcomes. A separate one-hourly session will be held to get to know you and to discuss this coaching agreement.

You may, if you wish, end the coaching sessions at any time, giving me one week's notice.

### Acceptance

As an indication of your acceptance of this coaching agreement and the terms mentioned within it, please sign and date below where appropriate and return this agreement to me.

Coach:

Date:

Coachee:

Date:

## Sample 2

### The purpose of a coaching agreement

This coaching agreement aims to set out clear definitions and expectations from both the coach and coachee prior to any coaching sessions taking place, so that both parties are aware of their individual responsibilities which foster an effective coaching relationship. This coaching agreement is intended as a guide and may, if necessary, be renegotiated by the coach during the course of the coaching relationship if in the best interests of the coachee.

Coaching works well when you:

- Are open and willing to consider change where this is necessary to aid development.
- Are open to new ways of learning and working which might challenge your thoughts and ideas.
- Are honest with your coach and yourself, particularly if you do not feel that something is working for you.
- Are ready to commit to your development by the giving and receiving of honest feedback.
- Recognise the investment being made in your development.
- Accept that commitment must first come from you before you can reap the benefits.

As your coach, I will endeavour to:

- Be focused on you and your best interests, which include your goals and your outcomes.
- Support and encourage you while you develop to your full potential.
- Be open, objective and non-judgemental, enabling you to set and work towards your own goals and achievements.
- Ask you questions that might challenge your ideas and thoughts as you progress and develop.
- Arrange a comfortable, private venue for our face-to-face discussions.

I look forward to coaching you and want you to be familiar with the following policies and procedures. If you have any questions, please contact me.

- **Procedure**: we will meet at the agreed time/date/location.
- **Coaching**: our agreement includes $x$ hours of face-to-face coaching per calendar month.
- **Changes**: if you need to reschedule a meeting, please give me at least one week's notice, if possible. If you have an emergency, we will work around it.
- **Extra time**: you may call or email me between our meetings if you need advice, have a problem or can't wait to share a success with me. This is included in your fee and is part of the support I offer. All I ask is that you keep the calls to 5–10 minutes each.
- **Records**: I usually ask that my coachees complete a prep form and send this via email 24 hours before each planned meeting/ call. This saves time and focuses our contact time but is optional.
- **Problems**: please use open and honest communication with me if you are not getting what you need from our coaching relationship. I will put your needs first every time.
- **Boundaries**: please note that coaching is not mentoring, counselling or therapy, and I will explain these differences if requested. If issues arise that we feel are not appropriate, I will be happy to refer you to a suitable professional.
- **Requests**: from time to time, I may challenge your thinking or behaviour. You are free to accept or decline these challenges. The purpose will always be to forward the action and deepen the learning.
- **Confidentiality**: all our sessions will remain totally confidential (unless otherwise agreed with the sponsor in consultation with the coach and coachee when contracting).

I am a member of the following professional organisations and adhere to their codes, standards and ethics: (Complete as appropriate.)

I confirm that I have read and agree to these client policies and procedures:

Client's signature:

Date:

Coach's signature:

Date:

## SAMPLE OF A COACHEE'S CASE NOTES

Name:

Address:

Age:

Start date:

No. of sessions:

Telephone nos.:

| Date | Summary of session | Agreed action/ goals | Coach's reflections |
|------|--------------------|--------------------|--------------------|
|      |                    |                    |                    |

## SAMPLE PREP FORM

Ideally, this form should be faxed, emailed or posted at least 48 hours before our agreed meeting/call each week. This will enable us to focus on the most important areas for you in any given week and will allow you to bring to the meeting/call those matters you feel are the most pressing.

Name:

Date:

Meeting/call time:

Call me on (insert tel. no.) for confirmation if required.

What I/we have achieved since our last meeting/call:

Commitments I/we made at the last meeting/call and actions taken:

What I/we would like to focus on today is:

## SAMPLE COACHING REVIEW FORM

(Complete halfway through the course of the coaching sessions and again at the end.)

Ideally this form should be faxed, emailed or posted to me at least 48 hours before our agreed meeting/call. This will enable us to review the sessions and prepare any report you may require for your organisation.

Name:

Date:

Meeting/call time:

Call me on (insert tel. no.) for confirmation if required.

What I have achieved since the start of coaching sessions:

What has been particularly helpful?

Commitments I made and follow-up action carried out as a result:

What I/we would like to focus on during the second half of the coaching programme is:

For the final session:

The main themes/focus of the sessions:

Key areas for further development and actions identified:

# EVALUATING YOUR COACH

Coach:

Coachee:

Date:

Give your coach some honest feedback on their performance.

| On a scale of 1–10, where 1 is poor and 10 is excellent, how well did your coach... | How do you know? |
|---|---|
| Create rapport? | |
| Listen and create a clear space for reflection? | |
| Use insightful questions? | |
| Reflect, reframe and clarify? | |
| Challenge and stretch? | |
| Get commitment/agree action? | |
| What would you have liked more of? | |

# THE INTERNATIONAL COACHING FEDERATION (ICF) CORE COACHING COMPETENCIES

A   SETTING THE FOUNDATION
1   Meeting ethical guidelines and standards
2   Establishing the coaching agreement

B   CO-CREATING THE RELATIONSHIP
3   Establishing trust and intimacy with the client
4   Coaching presence

C   COMMUNICATING EFFECTIVELY
5   Active listening
6   Powerful questioning
7   Direct communication

D   FACILITATING LEARNING AND RESULTS
8   Creating awareness
9   Designing actions
10  Planning and goal setting
11  Managing progress and accountability

(www.internationalcoachingfederation.org/uk)

# THE NATIONAL OCCUPATIONAL STANDARDS FOR COACHING AND MENTORING IN A WORK ENVIRONMENT DEFINITION OF COACHING

'Coaching in a work environment is defined within these standards as an ongoing professional relationship between the coach and the coachee that helps the coachee to:

- Clarify goals and aspirations and options for achieving them
- Improve their performance, skills and knowledge

■ To maximise their potential and personal development'

The standards state that the key values and principles of practitioners must be to:

■ 'Demonstrate empathy, sensitivity, compassion and respect
■ Be a self-reflective practitioner and undertake continuing professional development
■ Act in an open, honest and ethical way and agree those ethics with all relevant parties
■ Establish and maintain professional relationships with all key stakeholders to ensure no conflict of interest
■ Demonstrate a willingness to question own understanding, assumptions, beliefs and values
■ Respect boundaries and confidentiality
■ Demonstrate unwavering belief in the inherent potential of all individuals to learn, develop and achieve higher performance
■ Recognise that the responsibility to change lies with the coachee/mentee
■ Act in a way that balances the needs and interests of all stakeholders
■ Recognise the potential of all individuals to learn and develop
■ Value diversity in all its forms
■ Recognise the boundaries of coaching and/or mentoring and be aware that referral of the coachee/mentee may be necessary
■ Encourage the independence of the coachee/mentee'

**(http://www.ento.co.uk/standards/coaching_mentoring/)**

# Appendix 2

# Controlling costs

(This appendix is adapted and extended from Dembkowski *et al.*, 2006.)

There are significant returns for an organisation that maximises its leadership teams' performance through executive coaching. There has, however, been a lack of qualitative and quantitative measurements of the return on investment (ROI).

Before the coaching process, make sure clear objectives have been agreed by all the stakeholders. The questions to ask at this stage are as follows:

- What do you want to achieve from this coaching programme?
- What admin/reporting systems are in place to support the programme?
- What are the core values/behaviours that underpin this organisation?
- What are the specific organisational goals, team goals and individual goals?
- How will these goals benefit the three groups mentioned above?
- What do you expect from this programme that other interventions have not achieved?
- How will you measure the success of the programme?

After the halfway review, ask the following questions:

- How are the objectives/goals being met?
- On a scale of 1–10, how well are the sessions going?
- What is working well so far?
- What not working so well?
- What improvements/changes need to be made?

At the end of the programme, ask the following questions (these will vary according to organisation):

- What specifically has improved as a result of this programme, in terms of behaviours identified, performance, development, goals achieved?
- What are the key indicators (please tick those that apply)?
  - Increased motivation and confidence.
  - More ownership and responsibility for tasks and projects.
  - Enhanced leadership behaviours identified by organisation.
  - More effective delegation.
  - Greater confidence in management/leadership role.
  - Better reporting and communication.
  - Increased team productivity.
  - Enhanced quality of service or products.
  - Improved customer relations.
  - Reduction in delivery times.
  - Enhanced relationship with employees.
  - Enhanced relationship with boss/line manager.
  - Better worklife balance.
  - Less sick leave taken.
  - Reduced stress.
  - Staff retained for longer.
  - Fewer complaints.

For each of the ticked items above, complete a benefit calculation using Table 1.

Table 1.

| Indicator of impact | Estimated annual % improvement due | % confidence |
|---|---|---|
| | | |
| | | |
| | | |
| | | |
| | | |
| | | |
| | | |
| | | |
| | | |

When this table has been completed for all items, the monetary value can be calculated. Use the following formula:

Monetary value = Estimated annual monetary value of performance improvement × Estimated percentage improvement due to coaching × Percentage confidence in this estimate

Next, add up all the items to produce an overall sum. Check what intangible benefits you identified from the coaching programme. These can be handed to your coach to validate them with your organisation.

The coach should determine the costs of the coaching:

- Setting up and getting agreements.
- Fees charged.
- Client time to participate in coaching.
- Cover for client, if appropriate.
- Materials.
- Travel expenses.
- Admin costs.
- Telephone.

Add all the costs to produce a total figure. Now calculate the return on coaching investment:

(Benefits − Costs) × 100 = ROI

The critical success factors for demonstrating the ROI from coaching are as follows:

- SMART (**S**pecific, **M**easurable, **A**ttainable, **R**elevant, Time-bound) objectives and the benchmark for performance from existing appraisals and reviews.
- Ensuring that coaching objectives flow from the overall project objectives and/or business objectives.
- Communicating the methodology for measuring the monetary value of the coaching programme before the programme begins.
- Checking with the finance department for figures on client costs for participating in the coaching programme/sessions.
- Checking the costs of admin and support systems (360° assessments, etc.).
- Capturing both the tangible and intangible values of coaching.
- Communicating the results of the coaching programme to key stakeholders in the organisation.

- Sharing your findings with the coaching organisations, such as the Association for Coaching (AC), the International Coach Federation (ICF), the Institute of Leadership and Management (ILM) and the European Mentoring and Coaching Council (EMCC).

# Case studies and evidence to support the value of coaching

## CASE STUDIES

### Coaching in the private sector: Airbus

The question from the Human Resources (HR) Department in the autumn of 2001 was: 'What support can we offer to help our top managers succeed?' At the time, Airbus comprised four companies, of four different nationalities. Each member was responsible for manufacturing a part of the plane and for selling it to the others for the maximum profit. The challenge was to create *one* company, with one set of rules and shared values/behaviours.

In May 2000, HR carried out an assessment of 75 managers of the four nationalities, pre-selected for their technical and managerial competencies. The outcome of the assessment was that they chose 24 managers for 24 'new' key roles in *one* new company. Most of them had to move with their families from one country to another. They also had to put together a team of various European people whom they did not know.

The result of this assessment was the Airbus executive coaching programme. The overall purpose of this programme was to:

- accelerate the implementation and support for the new teams;
- build on common ground and promote cross-cultural understanding;
- develop leadership skills and enhance performance; and
- improve results for Airbus.

The areas addressed by the programme were chiefly to:

- support top people in tough jobs;
- strengthen key performers during critical times;
- enhance further the individuals' performance;
- create better leaders;
- reinforce a common leadership and results-focused culture in Airbus; and
- help embed identified Airbus key behaviours, working on how performers deliver, as well as what is delivered.

The communication 'strategy' and overall message were that coaching is:

- for the strong performers, recognising their achievement;
- a top-down process starting at executive level; and
- a gift from the company: promote it as such and use it to your own advantage.

## Implementation

First, a pilot project was run with 12 top managers. The results were considered positive, even though it was a short, three-month programme. The coaches' professionalism was recognised. As a result, the executive committee approved the launching of the programme on a larger scale.

*Enhance* (a Paris-based consultancy company) was given full responsibility for delivering the programme and for any issues or concerns that might arise. The coaches chosen had to meet Enhance's selection criteria:

- Fifteen years' minimum coaching at executive level in multi-cultural companies.
- Certified in their respective countries.
- International references.
- Multilingual.
- An ability to coach in their mother tongue and in English.

Participants were selected on the basis of the challenge of the new position, age, level of cultural integration, managerial credibility, past assessment/evaluation and potential for growth. They were invited to attend one of two kick-off meetings where the background and expectations for the programme were explained. This was followed by 15-minute individual interviews. The coachees were then asked to choose their two preferred coaches.

### Programme content

The programme content was as follows:

- A 360° feedback tool based on ten key leadership behaviours, selected by a team of 30 Airbus managers of various functions and nationalities. Each behaviour had four areas that were rated from one to five. This tool was available online and could be completed in 20 minutes. The coachees were asked to fill in the questionnaire and to request feedback from a minimum of five people to ensure the confidentiality of the feedback. The coaches were then given access to their coachees' overall results for use as support during the third coaching session.

- Telephone interviews conducted by the coach with four or five people selected by the coachees.
- One team observation meeting with the coach's silent presence. This enabled the coach to give their coachee feedback, if requested, and to coach them on their leadership 'presence'.
- Seven face-to-face coaching sessions of two hours without interruption, in a quiet place on site, over a period of approximate eight months.
- A confidential theme analysis conducted after the third session.
- A hot telephone line with the coach for one year.
- An action/leadership development plan shared with the operational manager and HR. This had the same format for every coachee but, when required, further actions were identified by the manager or HR. This document was confidential – it was the coachee's choice to share it with their manager and HR. Many did.
- Three months of telephone/email follow-up support.

The 360° feedback tool, telephone interviews and team observation meeting were very powerful in identifying gaps between the coachees' perceptions of themselves and others, and reality.

### Allocation of coaches

For each group of approximately 25 coachees, there were five coaches. They always respected the language in which the coachee wanted to be coached. They never had to reallocate someone, and they were always able to give the coachee one of their two preferred choices – and most of the time, their first. When they went into the fifth and sixth programmes, however, allocation became more delicate because sometimes the coaches had coached the managers in a previous programme. They had, therefore, with the agreement of the coachees, to get approval from their managers. In all cases, the rule was very simple: transparency, from all sides. If there was a doubt, no matter on which side, another coach would be allocated.

## Theme analysis

From my point of view as the project manager, the client was the company because the company pays the invoices – therefore Airbus had to be able to monitor and assess the results. From the coaches' point of view, the client was the coachee. We decided to inform Airbus about the overall progress of the work while at the same time totally respecting the confidentiality of the exchanges between the coach and coachee. To achieve this, between the third and fourth coaching session I had conference calls with the coaches, and they told me of the recurring themes they were working on with their coachees. No names were mentioned and so confidentiality was respected. On one programme we regularly found the same themes coming back, even when managers were of different nationalities in different locations.

This theme analysis, therefore, identified the following broad issues:

- Leadership skills and behaviours.
- The decision-making process.
- Empowerment.
- Stress and a work–life balance.
- Delegation.
- Effective communication.
- Self-marketing.

- Careers and promotion.
- Specific issues concerned with cross-cultural communication and culture clashes.

The report was sent to HR and the Cultural and Integration Vice-president and was also presented to the Executive Committee by HR.

My commitment to Airbus was then to:

- allocate the coaches/coachees within five days of the kick-off;
- distribute the CVs of individual coachees to the coaches;
- communicate all contact information to both the coach and coachees;
- ensure the coaches contacted their coachees and schedule as many sessions in advance as possible;
- organise the first face-to-face session as soon as possible;
- send an updated schedule to Airbus once a month for the full programme after ensuring every one was as aligned as far as possible; and
- ensure a harmonious and efficient roll-out.

## Outcomes

The results of coaching are difficult to measure in mathematical terms. In an unstable environment such as Airbus, this was not possible, so 'soft' criteria had to be relied on.

On the individual side:

- Those who were coached wanted their colleagues or sub-ordinates to be coached also and, very often, they suggested this should be by the same coach.
- The coachees often stayed in touch with their coaches once or

twice a year after the completion of the programme.

- When they were faced with a job change or a 'dimension' change in their responsibilities, they asked for a new coaching cycle.
- The coachees spoke openly about the outcome of their 360° feedback and asked for constructive feedback and coaching to enhance their behaviours.
- The 'de-dramatisation' of issues when the coachees realised that colleagues of other nationalities in different countries had the same problems.
- A better life balance, better stress management and the better delegation of tasks.

On the company side:

- The development of a more open culture of feedback.
- A strong team approach that developed links between managers.
- The accelerated integration and understanding of cultural differences.
- Help in stressful situations.
- The managers who were coached became better mentors, ensuring knowledge and experience would be passed on to younger managers.

Some individual coaching is still continuing, and team coaching – with a very operational, results-oriented approach – is being practised. The managers see their role as being their team's coach, and they are now successful at it.

## Conclusion

I always believe that coaching has been successful when it is not needed anymore. It is safe to say that Airbus (at the time of writing) is not there just yet. The executive coaching programme was/is very successful, but it is because of Airbus's complexity and their quest for excellence that support will continue. Airbus has demonstrated that coaching works for high achievers in a fast-paced environment.

(Ghislaine Gauthier, General Manager, Enhance, Paris)

## An organic and emergent approach to coaching

Six months on from our first coaching programme, coaching has had a significant impact on individual meetings with newly-appointed team leaders and group meetings, where particularly the use of specific coaching questions leads to greater effectiveness. I find as a manager, I am more effective at deep listening, and more aware of the kind of questions I ask, and their impact.

The specific behaviours/attitudes/situations which have benefited from coaching are a smarter working environment. We were always strong on positivity, but the coaching training has helped me to empower staff to achieve targets. My new team leaders are performing extremely well against the targets set out in their personal development reviews.

(Lucy Backhurst, Head of Undergraduate Recruitment and Admissions, Marketing and Communications Directorate, University of Newcastle upon Tyne)

## A tailored middle-ground approach to coaching

Kent County Council (KCC) approached Quality Education & Development Ltd (QED) to assist them in offering a coaching qualification to key people in the organisation. Initially we set up a pilot Institute for Leadership and Management (ILM) Level 5 Diploma programme for one group of people. This group comprised 14 managers. Each person was required to complete an assignment. Coral Ingleton, one of the group, and now Learning and Development Manager, used her assignment as the basis for her proposal, which was placed before senior management to support the development of a coaching culture across the organisation. The assignment proved to be the blueprint for the future development of the KCC coaching strategy. At the end of the programme, KCC referred QED to Kent Fire and Rescue Service, who were also considering coaching, and two ILM Level 3 Certificate in Coaching programmes were delivered to get things started there. This encouraged an atmosphere of collaboration and cross-county learning, which has been further developed in the intervening years.

By the end of 2008, KCC had trained almost 140 people to the ILM Level 5 standard and had introduced more than 140 other managers to the concepts of coaching through short courses for managers. In addition, coaching has become a feature of several other programmes provided by KCC for managers and staff. ILM programmes have included not only KCC staff, but also Kent Police and local voluntary sector staff. As the word spreads, the Kent Coaching Culture continues to grow.

In 2005, a KCC 'coaching network' was created by the original cohort of coaches. Now every coach is invited to join the network once they have achieved their qualification. The network's key purpose is to establish good practice in coaching across KCC and to provide an arena for the internal coaches to develop continuously.

Generally, managers have been supportive of those undertaking coaching and receiving coaching. The past five years have resulted in an awareness of the ethos of coaching, and there have been ever-increasing numbers of requests for coaches from the network, as well as evidence that managers are using coaching in their day-to-day roles.

Formal measurement of the impact of coaching has so far been somewhat limited. There is a lot of evidence of significant improvement in personal development. Coaching has encouraged managers to take time out to think things through. They have seen the potential that a coaching approach can bring.

### Environment and Regeneration Directorate

Katie Chantler has been instrumental in creating a 'coaching protocol' for the Environment and Regeneration Directorate. As one of the trained coaches, she tries to keep coaching within the directorate: keeping it local gives autonomy and independence. She says they are moving away from the concept that coaching someone too close in the organisational structure is a negative.

Before KCC offered coaching qualifications to its staff, the directorate utilised external coaches. They are still being used, especially by senior staff, but there is now an increased employment of internally-trained coaches. The directors have been openly supportive of coaching and had coaches themselves, which has helped the coaching culture. It is often the people who need coaching most who are most resistant to having coaching. Some staff also thought coaching expensive and time consuming and, with budget cuts, was considered a luxury. There was also a reluctance from some managers to allow staff access to coaching, as they thought it might take control away from them.

A recent leadership programme has helped to set a good example and overcome some of the barriers. Presentations are planned to inform managers that coaching can be considered alongside other development opportunities for staff. In the past, managers automatically sent staff on courses, but Katie wants to see coaching employed as an alternative or complementary option.

While the results have been difficult to quantify, there has been evidence that some staff who had considered moving on have been retained. There is now an atmosphere of openness and honesty, and evidence that managers are employing a 'coaching style' in their roles, being less directive and using questioning techniques. Katie acknowledges that formal evaluation is her next focus. She now has clearer expectations of coaches – internal and external – and will be focusing on ensuring that coaching is recorded in terms of hours and outcomes by all coaches.

The main impact of coaching appears to be that staff are feeling far more valued and appreciated. There has been a great deal of change in the directorate in recent years, which can lead to increased stress, yet staff say they feel 'looked after'.

## Schools Personnel Service

KCC's Schools Personnel Service has two qualified coaches. There is a strong awareness of the importance of well-being in this department and so both coaches have received specialist training in well-being coaching. For many coachees, the initial focus was on their well-being, and the first session involved a detailed health and well-being assessment before moving to more general coaching.

Nicky Whichelow, one of the coaches, has found some challenges, including not having enough time to meet demand. She has also had to ensure that the coachees' managers understand the confidential way in which coaches work and that managers are not party to any information from the sessions. Nicky has had to consider her agreements and how she involves line managers in this process. She has also experienced some people presenting for coaching when other support services were required, and she has been able to ensure that they access the appropriate options through the KCC Support Line.

Nicky keeps a diary of all her sessions, which has helped her to measure both her own development and her coachees' progress. She has used this to become more aware of any coaching 'habits' she has and says it has made her see more clearly her own 'filters'. It has helped her appreciate that staff are trying to do their very best at work, despite the challenges of their roles. It has also highlighted for her that not everyone is ready for coaching, and that this is a key area to investigate.

From the coaches' perspective, Nicky has noticed that 'leaders' who are coming up through KCC are seeking out coaching rather than training, to hone their skills and to help them to develop. It seems managers are also turning to coaching to help embed key behaviours and values.

(Julia Miles, Managing Director, QED)

## Using clean language (see page 73)

Lizz Clarke is the Managing Director of Logical Creative Marketing (LCM), a PR, marketing and design agency. She developed the business from a 'one-man band' to a company that employs 10 members of staff and has an annual turnover of nearly £1 million. I first coached Lizz (using clean language) five years ago. At this time she had two members of staff as well as people to whom she outsourced work. During one session, she spoke about being scatterbrained, and I asked a few questions to develop this metaphor:

'It's like there are scatters of seeds flying round in my head and I would like to feel more relaxed and in control. But it's like there's a small white fan whipping things up, fast and randomly. There could be between 10 and 50 seeds at any one time. And most of them are not labelled and a big seed could leap up and say, "You've got to do me tomorrow". I want to have a place for everything and everything in its place.'

These realisations led Lizz to make some changes and, in a subsequent session, Lizz told me:

'I love my seeds now. I know their names and where they are. And when there are some flying about, they are slightly bigger now and I can catch them. They take less than five minutes to list and everything I need is in a folder on my desk. I am also beginning to realise that other people can make them grow. I am nowhere near as worried about each day.'

And in the next session:

'I am worried about keeping this new pattern up. I am eager to find out how I can establish the new pattern. The seeds are still a little bit fly-away. They are not pinned down. There needs to be a link between the seeds and the core of the business. I need a landing stage. It's like I am growing the seeds into rush matting – but I can't stand and jump on it because it's not knitted together. I need to stop and knit it together. I need to think a bit more about what I've been doing, and put more bits of rush in. I could have more than one place where I can make seeds grow – so I can grow another bit of rush matting. I can see that there will be lots of stages: some small and some big, significant ones. I want it to be big, but I need to be secure on this stage first.'

I asked Lizz what needed to happen for the rush matting to grow bigger and for her to be more secure on this stage:

'I need to get more organised with communications in the office. I need to let some of the work go. I need to keep some kind of caring handle on it, but I don't need to know the detail. They need to feel I am interested. I need some way to monitor what's going on – we need a new accountancy firm with monthly reports so I can check what's happening. I need my staff to create weekly progress reports. I need a proper appraisal system. I want "corporate" rush matting.'

We discussed the above plans in more detail and, with this plan in place, Lizz felt she didn't need further coaching at that time. Recently, however, Lizz contacted me for another clean coaching session. At the start of the session, Lizz outlined three things that were on her mind:

- Developing a long-term vision and business strategy.
- Restructuring.
- Developing a score card for the business which will allow them to measure five or six things, constantly.

When I asked her what she would like to have happen, she envisioned a scenario where she doesn't do client work at LCM any more. Instead she chairs meetings where those who report to her come and tell her where they are on the score card, and they discuss deviations and what can be, or (ideally) is being, done about them. This is like being on the bridge of a ship, with five or six dials that let everyone know what adjustments to make. Getting the business 'shipshape' like this will allow Lizz to do what she really wants: put what she has learnt into practice with another business, invest in property and have time off.

As well as the 'ship' metaphor, two other metaphors appeared that warranted further exploration:

'I feel like the Incredible Hulk, stretching out of my clothes. I have been told about "letting go" by people; now I am beginning to know it. I can glimpse it and I am convinced that within a few months the picture will be clear.'

The Incredible Hulk represented thinking different things and old habits falling away. Lizz had got into a habit of hiding from going forward by busying herself with ironing and crosswords. She'd been complacent and had become uncomfortable with a feeling that everything was standing still. Now, she felt that freedom was coming. I asked where she felt that: 'It's coming into my head – a white/yellow light.' And where was it coming from? 'From the universe (she pointed up and in front of her), down and into the front of my head – just going in and cleaning bits up.'

Lizz experienced the light as powerful, giving and gushing: 'Oh! I can't take it in all at once. It will sweep me away...I need to be able to control it – and I can control it.' How did Lizz know she could control it? 'All I have to do is turn my face away from the light and take a rest.' This would involve ironing and crosswords – and long soaks in the bath – but now it wouldn't be mindless hiding, it would have a purpose...to rest from the light. 'And I won't be doing it much.'

And when a light could go into her head and clean bits up, what kind of 'clean bits up' was that?

'Exhausting. I have to spend a lot of time with people with more expertise than me, them explaining so I can see things more clearly, and it can be arduous. The meeting I had yesterday (where explaining was happening) was like wading through treacle. There have been challenges all my life, but this is different. I have to understand detailed concepts and then apply them to help other people to change their behaviour. But the glimpse of the picture keeps me going.'

Where was the glimpse?

'To the right and up. I am not looking at the glimpse for a picture. Oh, that is where the light is coming from (not ahead). I am pulling it into me. It is tiring and exhausting. It is half good and half bad. I am excited by the knowledge, but frightened by the arduousness of it.'

So when it's half good and half bad, what would Lizz like to have happen?

'I'd rather like it if I could be more in control of the cycle. And I'd like to tidy up my personal life, too. My home, my physical fitness. As I stretch, the light is coming in and it's not all for work. I want to support my son better. I could use the five dials for home things as well. When I was pushing the company ahead before, I could always fit things in: I had lots of energy.'

Although the metaphors were different, it seemed to me as if there were some similarities between Lizz's current situation and what we had been discussing five years ago. Both times, Lizz was talking about 'bits' in her mind, and both times she was envisioning building a bigger business and letting go. (I was able to recall this because metaphors are very memorable and capture the structure of someone's thought processes rather than the content.) So I asked Lizz whether there was a relationship between the light and the rush matting:

'Yes, there is. The rush matting is now very firm. I have built lots of steps since then, and they are solid. I am not worried about the next step. I know I can build it. They (the people who work in the company) are building it. They build it for me to walk on. I think I need to give them the rush matting pattern. What they are building is solid but not pretty. They are each building their own bit, and the bits are solid, the joins are fairly solid, but it could fall apart. I need them all to do the score card pattern. And creating a vision is the context for the pattern. It is like when you buy a duvet cover and, in the corner of the packaging, there's a picture of how the whole cover looks on the bed: you can see the whole thing and the pattern. And everyone else can see it as well. When we are two or three steps further up, the rush matting and the pattern is strong, the company will be able to live on in its own right.'

Lizz was already working on the score card and so needed to continue with that and with her long-term business strategy and restructuring. So what difference did this session make to Lizz?

'Now I know where the light is, it feels like an entity and that I have some control over it. I can turn away from it and I can decide to let some light in. The meeting I went to yesterday felt like I was swimming in treacle; it was hard to move forward. Now I will think of meetings like that as "light meetings". I will just let the light in. And I can have light time anywhere – at my PC, for example. The study is full of clutter and the room is dark and dingy but if I allow the light to flood in, it gives me energy. That's the main difference. I was feeling a bit hopeless and depressed. Then I went to the light – and it lit everything. I will have energy for my home, my physical fitness, my family and my work.'

Within a week of the session, Lizz contacted me to tell me that she had:

- a tidy home office;
- sorted out her son's homework schedule;
- had an induction session at a gym two minutes' walk away from her main office;
- had two discussions with one of the people that she previously felt exhausted by and both times had felt energised instead.

'I am about to go into another of this sort of meeting and I realise my attitude is very enthusiastic rather than "girding my loins", so I imagine the outcome will be different. Its amazes me how much personal development I have done and how, each time I reach a new platform of success, I need to learn anew!'

(Marion Way, Clean Coach/Trainer)

## EVIDENCE TO SUPPORT THE VALUE OF COACHING

'Coaching has made staff feel valued during a period of uncertainty and much change.'

(Leanne McMahon, Control Room Manager,
Kent Fire and Rescue Service)

'The fire service is currently undergoing its biggest period of change since its formation in 1947. Coaching has been identified as one of the most effective ways of supporting this change, as well as helping to facilitate new projects, improve job satisfaction and morale, reduce conflict and stress and improve self-management.'

(Dean Firmin, Kent Fire and Rescue Service)

'Coaching has led me to view every facet of life as a mirror in which an image is reflected and is entirely controlled by an individual's perception. In short the image will be whatever you allow it to be.'

(Tim Gibson, Head of Command and Operational Training,
Kent Fire and Rescue Service)

'It has, for me, reinforced the value of listening skills and the pride you can get by allowing the coachee to actually develop themselves.'

(John Ripley, Training Centre Manager,
Kent Fire and Rescue Service)

'Coaching has really changed how I upward manage, and empowered me to challenge senior management. I no longer avoid conflict, and am able to give positive feedback and support my team more easily.'

(Jon Chambers, Senior Executive of IT,
company based in Surrey)

'I want our school to become a coaching community because I see many benefits. It encourages trust and sharing. It will energise staff and get them to feel enthusiastic about their work and enjoy it again – by giving them the opportunity to take control and choose their own direction. Also, I do think it helps us see what we're doing well – which we're bad at doing... It will make us more cohesive as a school and more of a community. And I believe it will empower our middle managers by giving them the tools and confidence to lead the staff in their department forward. Ultimately the knock-on effect will be in quality of teaching and learning.'

(Rose Finch, Assistant Head, Sir Charles Parsons School and Science College, Newcastle upon Tyne)

'Since starting the coaching programme, I have found that staff are more organised, generally. They seem to plan better and return work on time. The change in their attitude towards customers has improved significantly.'

(Accounts Manager, Barclays Bank)

'Developing coaching skills for all our staff, as a framework for professional conversations, is a School Improvement Plan leadership priority next year.'

(David Pearmain, Head Teacher, Kenton School, Newcastle upon Tyne)

'I see coaching as a crucial tool for personal and professional development and for working with individuals. It develops leadership at all levels – tapping into individual potential of each member of your team. The fact that you've got more motivated staff with better-developed skills means the knock-on effect is in quality and emotional engagement – and in better learning. Teachers are leaders too so they can use some of the skills in relating with young people directly.'

(Ian Lane, Senior School Improvement Adviser, Local Authority, Newcastle upon Tyne)

'With a successful coaching relationship you can progress through tasks more easily and successfully, so you get more personal satisfaction. Teachers and support staff being more at ease with their workload will be reflected in their relationships with young

people and ultimately in improved teaching and learning.'
> (Sue Blakemore, Aimhigher and G & T Co-ordinator,
> Local Authority, Newcastle upon Tyne)

'Coaching came along at exactly the right time for me. It provided me with a framework and context to be the type of manager I want to be, integrating what I already knew with development of new skills.'
> (Sam Sheppard, Kent County Council)

Finally, a survey of 735 managers by the Roffey Park Institute found that 70% were looking for a greater sense of meaning in their working lives. This was articulated as:

- connecting with others;
- having a sense of personal purpose;
- a heightened understanding of what is really important to be human;
- a sense of community.

# Useful resources

## BIBLIOGRAPHY AND REFERENCES

Argyris, C. and Schön, D. (1978) *Organizational Learning: A Theory of Action Perspective*. Menlo Park, CA: Addison-Wesley.

Arnold, J. (2008) *Teach Yourself Speaking on Special Occasions*. London: Hodder Education.

Association for Coaching (2006) *Value of Coaching*. London: AC.

Bradford, D. and Cohen, A. (1998) *Power Up: Transforming Organisations through Shared Leadership*. Chichester: Wiley.

Chartered Institute of Personnel and Development (2004) *Guide to Coaching*. London: CIPD.

Chartered Institute of Personnel and Development (2007) *Developing Coaching Capability in Organisations*. London: CIPD.

Cooperrider, D. (1990) *Appreciative Inquiry in Organizational Life*.

Cooperrider, D. and Srivastia (1987) *Positive Image, Positive Action*.

Dembkowski, S., Eldridge, F. and Hunter, I. (2006) *The Seven Steps of Effective Executive Coaching*. London: Thorogood Publishing.

Gallwey, Tim, see **http://www.theinnergame.com**

Gerber, Michael, E. see **http://www.e-myth.com**

Goleman, D. (2006) *Emotional Intelligence and Social Intelligence*. London: Hutchinson.

Grove, David, J. (1991) *Metaphors to Health & In the Presence of the Past*. ELDON M.

Halpern, B.L. and Lubar, K. (2003) *Leadership Presence*. New York, NY: Gotham Books.

Hawkins, P. and Shohet, R. (2000) *Supervision in the Helping Professions*. Maidenhead: Open University Press.

Hay, J. (2007) *Reflective Practice and Supervision for Coaches*. London: Karnac Books.

IPMA (2001) International Personnel Management Association Research. (Jan.) See **www.impa-hr.org**

Jarvis, J., Lane, D.A. and Fillery-Travis, A. (2006) *The Case for Coaching*. London: CIPD.

Klein, N. (1999) *Time to Think*. London: Ward Lock.

Kolb, D. (1984) *Experiential Learning*. Englewood Cliffs, NJ: Prentice Hall.

Lawley, J. and Tompkins, P. (2000) *Metaphors in Mind*. Development Company Press.

Luft, J. (1969) *Of Human Interaction*. Palo Alto, CA: National Press.

Murdoch, Edna. See **www.coachingsupervisionacademy.com**

O'Neill, M.B. (2000) *Executive Coaching with Backbone and Heart*. San Francisco, CA: Jossey Bass.

Senge, P. (2006) *Presence*. New York, NY: Currency.

Stephenson, P. (2000) *Executive Coaching*. Englewood Cliffs, NJ: Prentice Hall.

Tolle, E. (2004) *The Power of Now*. Novato, CA: New World Library.

Way, Marian, Clean language coach and trainer. See **www.apricotisland.com.**

Whitmore, J. (2002) *Coaching for Performance*. London: Nicholas Brealey.

## WEBSITES

Author's own
**www.coach4executives.com** and **www.able2speak.com**
Association for Coaching
(**http://www.associationforcoaching.com**)

Chartered Institute of Personnel and Development
   (**http://www.cipd.co.uk/**)
Coach University USA
   (**www.coachu.com**)
Coaching UK
   (**http://www.coaching-uk.org.uk/**)
European Coaching Institute
   (**www.europeancoachinginstitute.org**)
European Mentoring and Coaching Council
   (**http://www.emcouncil.org/**)
Institute of Leadership and Management
   (**http://www.i-l-m.com**)
International Coach Federation UK
   (**http://www.coachfederation.org.uk**)
International Coach Federation USA
   (**http://www.coachfederation.org**)
Mirus Coaching for Social Change
   (**www.miruscoaching.org**)

# Index